W9-BTM-182

Biblical Prophecy

Zondervan Quick-Reference Library

Biblical Archaeology
Biblical Prophecy
The Books of the Bible
Christian Theology
Early Church History
How We Got the Bible
The Life of Christ
Old Testament History

ZONDERVAN
QUICK
REFERENCE
LIBRARY

Biblical Prophecy

John H. Sailhamer

ZondervanPublishingHouse
Grand Rapids, Michigan

A Division of HarperCollinsPublishers

Biblical Prophecy
Copyright © 1998 by John H. Sailhamer

Requests for information should be addressed to:

📖 ZondervanPublishingHouse
Grand Rapids, Michigan 49530

Library of Congress Cataloging-in-Publication Data

Sailhamer, John.
  Biblical prophecy / John H. Sailhamer.
     p.   cm. — (Zondervan quick reference library)
   ISBN: 0-310-50051-6 (softcover)
   1. Bible—Prophecies. I. Title. II. Series.
BS647.2.S25   1998
220.1'5—dc21   97-45991
                                                          CIP

All Scripture quotations, unless otherwise indicated, are taken from the *Holy Bible: New International Version*®. NIV®. Copyright © 1973, 1978, 1984 by International Bible Society. Used by permission of Zondervan Publishing House. All rights reserved.

All rights reserved. No part of this publication may be reproduced, stored in a retrieval system, or transmitted in any form or by any means—electronic, mechanical, photocopy, recording, or any other—except for brief quotations in printed reviews, without the prior permission of the publisher.

Interior design by Sue Vandenberg Koppenol

Printed in the United States of America

---

99 00 01 02 03 04 /❖ DC/ 10 9 8 7 6 5 4 3 2

Contents

Abbreviations of the Books of the Bible

Genesis	Gen.	Nahum	Nah.
Exodus	Ex.	Habakkuk	Hab.
Leviticus	Lev.	Zephaniah	Zeph.
Numbers	Num.	Haggai	Hag.
Deuteronomy	Deut.	Zechariah	Zech.
Joshua	Josh.	Malachi	Mal.
Judges	Judg.	Matthew	Matt.
Ruth	Ruth	Mark	Mark
1 Samuel	1 Sam.	Luke	Luke
2 Samuel	2 Sam.	John	John
1 Kings	1 Kings	Acts	Acts
2 Kings	2 Kings	Romans	Rom.
1 Chronicles	1 Chron.	1 Corinthians	1 Cor.
2 Chronicles	2 Chron.	2 Corinthians	2 Cor.
Ezra	Ezra	Galatians	Gal.
Nehemiah	Neh.	Ephesians	Eph.
Esther	Est.	Philippians	Phil.
Job	Job	Colossians	Col.
Psalms	Ps(s).	1 Thessalonians	1 Thess.
Proverbs	Prov.	2 Thessalonians	2 Thess.
Ecclesiastes	Eccl.	1 Timothy	1 Tim.
Song of Songs	Song	2 Timothy	2 Tim.
Isaiah	Isa.	Titus	Titus
Jeremiah	Jer.	Philemon	Philem.
Lamentations	Lam.	Hebrews	Heb.
Ezekiel	Ezek.	James	James
Daniel	Dan.	1 Peter	1 Peter
Hosea	Hos.	2 Peter	2 Peter
Joel	Joel	1 John	1 John
Amos	Amos	2 John	2 John
Obadiah	Obad.	3 John	3 John
Jonah	Jonah	Jude	Jude
Micah	Mic.	Revelation	Rev.

Introduction

What Is This Book?

The *Zondervan Quick-Reference Library: Biblical Prophecy* is a new and unique reference tool. Simply put, it is a complete and succinct commentary on the prophetic element of the Bible; each unit of this discussion you can read approximately in one minute. You do not need to wade through a lot of information, for this book goes right to the point—the exposition of the major issues of biblical prophecy itself. It not only takes into account the latest in biblical scholarship, it also shows the sense and place each prophecy occupies within the larger structure of the whole Bible.

Because we get so much of our information in daily life quickly and efficiently, we are becoming increasingly accustomed to having information or knowledge about the Bible given to us in the same way. Though the need for fast delivery systems often undercuts the role of thoughtful reflection in our society, our habits have changed. We have adjusted to the routines of everyday life around us. There is therefore a legitimate need for a more efficient way to build our knowledge of the Bible and its content—if only as a starting point for more in-depth and reflective understanding. It is a truism in learning that once we get a sense of what a particular Bible theme is about, the details of that theme make more sense.

A regular use of the *Zondervan Quick-Reference Library: Biblical Prophecy* should lead to a more knowledgeable study of God's Word and of prophecy in particular. It can, of course, be used along with traditional Bible study tools, and this book is not intended to replace them. Rather, our aim is to supply the legitimate need (or appetite) for efficiency in obtaining Bible knowledge. It is a convenient starting point.

The *Zondervan Quick-Reference Library: Biblical Prophecy* has two distinct features: (1) a series of introductory pages, intended to bring the reader up to speed on the study of Bible prophecy; (2) a series of brief comments on all the major prophetic elements of the Bible. Each page, which covers a single topic of biblical prophecy, is intended to be read on its own. The book as a whole may also be read consecutively to obtain a complete picture of what the Bible says about the prophetic future.

Introduction to Bible Prophecy

Christians and Bible Prophecy

Immediately after Jesus' ascension, two angels appeared to the disciples and told them, "This same Jesus, who has been taken from you into heaven, will come back in the same way you have seen him go into heaven" (Acts 1:11). Since then, Christians have been watching and waiting for Christ's return. This is the most common experience of Christians everywhere.

But the idea of Christ's return has also been a stumbling block to true faith. Many modern Christians find it hard to believe that Jesus will return to this earth. To believe that he will physically return to this earth and reign as king stretches their faith almost to the breaking point. Moreover, countless Christians have attempted to second-guess Christ's coming by setting dates. Those dates have come and gone, but Jesus has not returned. To many that is a sign that Jesus will perhaps never come. They forget that Jesus himself said, "It is not for you to know the times or dates [of my return and my kingdom]" (Acts 1:7).

Already in the first century, Christians began to grow impatient and needed constant reminders of the reality of Christ's return. Peter, a disciple who was present at Christ's ascension and who had seen a "preview" of his return on the Mount of Transfiguration (Matt. 17:1–13; 2 Peter 1:18), has given the church a succinct and valuable reminder. He focuses his own last words to the church on this issue (2 Peter 3:1–18). We would do well to bear in mind a few key ideas from this passage. (1) Peter grounds his hope in Christ's return in the predictions of the holy prophets and in the Lord's teaching preserved by the apostles (3:2)—that is, the Old and New Testaments. Our hope in Christ's return should be grounded in Scripture. Earlier Peter has reminded us that we must base our hope of Christ's return on what he calls "the word of the prophets made more certain" (1:19). Our hope must be based on the Scriptures, not on speculations, nor dreams and visions, nor any new prophecies.

(2) The biblical view of our Lord's return is grounded in the doctrine of creation. God created the world out of nothing; he will reduce it to nothing and create it anew (2 Peter 3:5–7). Biblical prophecy is about reclaiming God's good creation.

(3) The Lord is deliberately postponing his return out of a deep mercy for those who will be left behind. He does not want anyone to perish. But when he does return, it will be like a thief in the night—suddenly and unexpectedly.

(4) In our waiting for the Lord's return we must be occupied in living a righteous life, corresponding to the righteousness that awaits us in the new heavens and new earth. The goal of studying Bible prophecy should always be godly living, "while we wait for the blessed hope—the glorious appearing of our great God and Savior, Jesus Christ" (Titus 2:13).

History of Interpretation of Bible Prophecy

In the early centuries of the church, most Christians looked for Christ to return and reign here on earth (millennialism). As the church grew more powerful and became a social and political institution, the hope in Christ's return to establish his kingdom was refocused on the church itself, and the church was identified with the kingdom of God (amillennialism). The church taught that all believers had been resurrected from spiritual death when they were baptized, and virtually all Bible prophecies were understood as fulfilled in the life of the present church. Prophecies were thus interpreted "spiritually."

In our day, Bible prophecies are once again being studied for what they tell us about the Lord's actual return, but in a way different from the past. This intense interest in and anticipation of the return of Christ began to grow in earnest some two hundred years ago, for at least three reasons. (1) In the eighteenth century, a strong reaction in the churches developed to the prevailing idealism in Christian theology. Theology was little more than a study of human ideas about God and the world. Theologians treated the Bible as a kind of storybook of illustrations of human ideas about God. In reaction, pastors and teachers began to stress that the Bible was about "real things" and "real people," not just ideas. When it spoke about the past, it was concerned with real events. So also, when it spoke about the future (prophecy), it was also concerned about real events, real people, and real time. When people began reading the Bible that way, they became interested in what was going to happen in the future—"in the last days." What were the future events about which the Bible spoke?

(2) The eighteenth century also saw a great rise in biblicism—the belief that the Bible alone, not the church creeds, represented the only guide for Christian living. This led to the development of a renewed interest in those books of the Bible that had been largely ignored because they contained little that was in the creeds. Prophetic books like Ezekiel, Daniel, Zechariah, and Revelation gained new prominence. The Bible was like a new frontier.

(3) In the late eighteenth century, time was beginning to run out on traditional prophetic chronologies. Many chronological systems of the early medieval church that were used to predict the coming of the Antichrist were coming due. In the early Middle Ages, for example, the crowning of Charlemagne on Christmas day, A.D. 800, was seen as the beginning of the millennial (thousand-year) reign of Christ over the church. On that chronological scheme, great expectations arose as the year 1800 approached (see next section). The one thousand years of Christ's reign through the church and Western society were coming to an end. Could this mean that Christ himself would soon appear?

A Convergence of Historical Events

The one thousand years since the beginning of the Holy Roman Empire in A.D. 800 was coming to a close in the late eighteenth century. People began to expect that the Antichrist would soon make himself known, which would mean a breakdown of Christian society. The medieval monarchies that had governed Europe would fall apart, the common people would take over control of government (democracy), chaos would ensue, and the Antichrist would appear to restore order. He would raise a mighty army and launch an attack against God's people and the Holy Land. Such was the thinking at the beginning of the last century.

Precisely at this same time in world history, three major historical events converged: (1) the European intellectual movement called "The Enlightenment," which represented the rise of humanism and a severe attack on Christianity; (2) the French Revolution, which resulted in the fall of the European monarchies (which had been identified with the millennial reign of Christ) and the rise of democracy; (3) the rise of Napoleon I, who raised a mighty army, restored order, and launched an attack against Protestant Europe and the remnants of the Holy Roman Empire, the church, and the Holy Land. Napoleon did exactly what had been expected of the Antichrist. Most Bible-believing Christians in those days felt strongly that Napoleon was the Antichrist.

Many at that time believed that the church would defeat the Antichrist and usher in a second millennium, which would end with the return of Christ (postmillennialism). When the Protestant countries of northern Europe did defeat Napoleon, a new optimism for bringing in the kingdom of God began to flourish. But as the century wore on, that optimism began to wane. Liberalism, on the other hand, continued to increase its own optimistic millennial hopes that things were getting better and better. By the end of the nineteenth century, the millennialism of classical liberalism attached itself to such utopian schemes as communism, socialism, and nationalism.

The increasingly pessimistic evangelical millennialism, on the other hand, became almost completely "premillennial"—the belief that Christ would have to return to earth before the Millennium. They believed human society, rather than getting better on its own, was in fact getting worse.

The publication of the Scofield Reference Bible (1909) represents a defining moment in the development of modern premillennialism. In the midst of the great optimism of pre-World War I America and Europe, the editors of the Scofield Bible maintained that the world was not going to get better in this century. This was not going to be a "Christian century," as so many in that day believed. According to Scofield, the mixture of iron and clay in the feet of the great statue in Nebuchadnezzar's dream meant that the "Gentile world-system" would grow progressively weaker and more chaotic. All this led to an increased expectation of the return of Christ. It has continued into the second half of the present century.

The Return of the Jews to Palestine

One of the key stumbling blocks to a realistic reading of biblical prophecy has always been the scriptural notion of the return of the Jews to Palestine, the "Promised Land" (e.g., Ezek. 36:24). In the medieval period, biblical texts that spoke explicitly of the Jews' return to their homeland were frequently used by Jewish apologists in their debates with Christians. They argued that if Jesus were the Messiah and the church his kingdom (as the church itself maintained), then why were the Jews not living in the Promised Land? Was not that what the Bible promised? For well over one thousand years the Jews had not lived in their homeland, nor was it likely to happen, they maintained. This seemed to present an almost insurmountable obstacle to believing the literal promise of the Lord's return. In response to this obstacle, many Jewish mission organizations were organized during the nineteenth century. In some measure these were intended to hasten the return of the Lord.

In the twentieth century, however, all that changed. The seemingly impossible happened; the Jews did return to their homeland—aided by, of all things, the British empire! Curiously enough, British theologians had long maintained that the United Kingdom would play a central role in the restoration of the Jews to their land. Since the miraculous defeat of the Spanish Armada in 1588, which to many in Britain represented the defeat of the Roman Catholic Church, British theologians had argued from Bible prophecy that their nation was God's "elect nation." In Ezekiel 38:13, for example, "Tarshish and her strong lions" (NIV note) was identified as the British empire, whose symbol was a lion. Britain, they believed, would be God's instrument in restoring the kingdom of God and returning the Jews to their land.

During World War I, the British Prime Minister David Lloyd George was the only member of the government who wanted to acquire Palestine as a Jewish homeland. Through his instigation in 1917, the Balfour Declaration, granting Jews the right to a homeland in Palestine, was signed. Why did this man, against the advice of his own cabinet, shape British foreign policy around the idea of the Jews' return to Palestine? According to David Fromkin, *A Peace to End All Peace*, Lloyd George "was not, like ... the other members of the Cabinet, educated in an exclusive public school that stressed the Greek and Latin classics; he was brought up on the Bible. ... Unlike his colleagues he was keenly aware that there were centuries-old tendencies in British Nonconformist and Evangelical thought toward taking the lead in restoring the Jews to Zion" (pp. 267–68).

In the twentieth century, the world's attention has focused on the Middle East, making the subject of Bible prophecy almost unavoidable to the biblical Christian.

Hermeneutics of Bible Prophecy

Biblical Realism

The biblical authors were realists. In Scripture they present a realistic view of God and the world, and they want this world to be taken at face value. In interpreting these biblical texts, however, not everyone reads them with the same focus on their realism. The Bible and the events depicted in it have been viewed in at least three ways.

(1) *The mythological approach to the Bible.* Many today hold that the biblical texts do not record real events; rather, they are mere stories, intended to illustrate or teach religious ideas. According to this view, the narrative of Genesis 1, for example, does not give details of God's creative acts, but only the fact that God created the universe. Its main teaching is that the world is a suitable place for us to live. In other words, biblical narratives are largely "mythical." They focus on important lessons for life, and we should not get caught up in the details of the narrative.

(2) *Naturalism.* For others, the Bible is about real events, but it does not record them exactly as they happened. Rather, they believe it embellishes them with divine actions and miracles, and naturalism searches for the natural explanation behind the events. According to this view, behind the creation narrative in Genesis 1 lies a completely naturalistic account of the origin of the world. Terms such as "day" must be understood in the geological sense of an eon of thousands or millions of years. Behind the ostensibly miraculous events in the Bible stand natural occurrences. When the Bible says the Nile turned to blood (Ex. 7:20), the naturalist believes it means that it became reddish in color because of a overabundant growth of microorganisms in the water.

(3) *Biblical realism.* In this third view, the Bible records real events. Things happened just as they are recounted in the Bible. Supernatural events happened supernaturally. Genesis 1 records what actually happened. When applied to biblical prophecy, biblical realism believes that future events are also described in the Bible just as they will happen. That is, both future events and past events are recounted realistically—though one must remain sensitive to the various types of literature used by the biblical authors to depict future events (see next section).

Literary Types in Prophetic Literature

In this book we will be taking a realistic view of biblical prophecy. That does not mean, however, that we can overlook the fact that in their visions of the future, the prophets drew heavily from various kinds of literature. They intended to depict a real world, but they did not always use literature that was meant to be taken literally. A realistic reading of the Bible, in other words, does not entail a strictly literal one. In interpreting prophecy, we must be careful both to read the Bible realistically and to understand the scope of the kind of literature used by the biblical authors. The prophets used three basic kinds of literature.

(1) *Poetic literature.* Poetry was the primary means the prophets used to develop their major themes. Biblical poetry has three basic characteristics. (a) Poetry is *figurative.* It uses such figures of speech as images, similes, and metaphors to convey its ideas. The prophet Habakkuk, for example, uses a simile to describe God's protective care when he says, "He makes my feet like the feet of a deer" (Hab. 3:19). (b) Biblical poetry is *complex*, meaning that it does not always render a single, unified picture of reality. Poetry often gives only bits and pieces of the reality it is portraying, and each bit must be appreciated individually. In the second half of the poetic line in Habakkuk 3:19, for example, the prophet says of God, "He enables me to go on the heights." We should not read this poetic line as saying, "He has made me like deer's feet on the heights." The image of "deer's feet" (meaning swiftness) must not be joined to "walking on the heights" (meaning power and agility). (3) Biblical poetry is to be read according to *biblical realism.* Though it uses figurative language, it is about real persons and things.

(2) *Narrative literature.* Biblical narratives record real history, whether from the past or in the future, and they should be read literally. What God promised in the past often forms the basis of his future actions. When biblical narratives recount God's promises, we should expect those promises to be carried out realistically and literally. When the promises are made to Israel, for example, we should expect them to be fulfilled for Israel. If David was promised a literal eternal kingdom in Jerusalem, then we should expect the same of its fulfillment.

(3) *Apocalyptic literature.* A third type of biblical literature found in prophetic texts, called "apocalyptic literature," was developed specifically by the biblical authors to present their major themes. Because of the prominence of this type of literature in prophetic texts, we will discuss it at length in the next section.

Apocalyptic Literature

Apocalyptic literature is a highly symbolic form of historical narrative. Real events are depicted in detailed symbolic language. Usually these aspects of apocalyptic literature are developed within a narrative by means of dreams and visions. In the book of Daniel, for example, the historical narrative of Daniel's dream begins like any other biblical narrative: "In the first year of Belshazzar king of Babylon, Daniel had a dream, and visions passed through his mind as he was lying on his bed" (Dan. 7:1). What follows, however, contains every form of apocalyptic symbolism. Daniel sees, for example, "the four winds of heaven churning up the great sea. Four great beasts, each different from the others, came up out of the sea" (7:2–3).

Because of their dual nature, both literal and symbolic, biblical apocalyptic texts require careful interpretation. Such texts should be understood realistically, but not literally. Revelation 19:11–15, for example, says that when Christ returns, he will be riding on "a white horse" and will defeat Satan and his hosts with a "sharp sword" that comes out of his mouth. What does this depict? There will be a real battle between Christ and Satan, and Satan will literally be defeated. But will Christ actually ride on a white horse? Will he literally slay the nations by means of a sword that comes out of his mouth? An appreciation of the symbolic nature of this vision/narrative suggests that it need not be taken literally. Similarly regarding the "bottomless pit" in 20:3 (RSV): Is this a real pit without a bottom? Probably not. This is symbolic, but the symbol stands for a real place where Satan will be bound.

How, then, do we interpret the symbolic language of apocalyptic texts? (1) Apocalyptic texts usually provide their own interpretation. Daniel himself, for example, was perplexed at the meaning of his visions and had to ask an angel for their interpretation (Dan. 7:15–16); the angel's interpretation is given in the text. (2) Apocalyptic texts usually draw on events depicted literally elsewhere in the Bible. God's promises to Israel, clearly laid out in biblical narratives, are given their fulfillment in apocalyptic literature. The symbols of those texts are about the literal fulfillment of God's promises recorded in the narratives. (3) Apocalyptic texts are often explained in later biblical books. Daniel, for example, is explained in the book of Revelation.

Apocalyptic literature is written to give hope for the future, not information about the future. Biblical apocalyptic texts are not predictive prophecy. They are, rather, symbolic narratives, intended to give us a picture of what the future holds, but without the specific details of its fulfillment. The details come only after the actual real events occur.

Time Predictions

Both Jews and Christians have devoted much effort to predicting the exact time of the Messiah's coming. Underlying these attempts are three distinct approaches. (1) A *"six thousand year" scheme of world history.* This approach assumes the world will last only six thousand years, after which the Messiah will come and reign another thousand years (the Millennium). Underlying this approach is an ancient chronological view that dates the creation of the world at around 4000 B.C. Needless to say this view is receiving a great deal of interest as the twentieth century heads towards the year 2000. Support for this view, however, is hard to find in Scripture. The best that can be done is to argue that the six days of creation in Genesis 1 each somehow correspond to a thousand years—note Peter's statement, "With the Lord a day is like a thousand years" (2 Peter 3:8). Furthermore, the biblical genealogies were not intended as chronologies; thus many more actual years have most likely transpired since creation.

(2) *Identifying the Antichrist and thus predicting the coming of Christ.* Many biblical scholars, recognizing that the Bible does not give grounds for identifying the exact time of the return of Christ, turn their attention to predicting the time of the Antichrist. The idea behind this approach is that if we can identify his appearance in our own times, then the Lord's return must be near. The problem with this assumption is that the Bible teaches that "many antichrists" are in the world and have been since the first days of the church (1 John 2:18).

(3) *Identifying the time of the "last generation" (Matt. 24:3–35) by means of "signs of the times."* Though we may not be able to predict the exact time of Christ's return, many suppose we can look for "signs" that support the assumption that the end is near. This is a popular approach today, for many events in this century appear to be of prophetic importance. But the problem with this approach lies in the inherent difficulties of linking biblical apocalyptic images and symbols to actual events. The biblical images appear often in poetic texts and are thus open to various interpretations. If we get specific, we raise the chances of miscalculation.

What we can do, however, is to look for increasing convergence of world events and biblical themes—for example, Israel's return to Palestine; war and peace in the Middle East; growing apostasy in the professing church; movement toward a one-world government; an increasing fragmentation of society (iron and clay); growth in world missions and evangelism. These are all events that appear to be taught in biblical prophetic texts. The convergence of these prophetic events in our time suggests that God's Word is still on target and that Christ's return is near.

Biblical Theological Foundations
of Bible Prophecy

The Biblical Idea of Creation

The Bible teaches that God is the Creator and Sustainer of the world. In technical language this is known as *theism*. Theism is the belief in a living, personal, good God, who is distinct from the world but actively involved in it. This view is set forth clearly in Genesis 1. In verse 1, we find the notion of "creation out of nothing" (i.e., *ex nihilo*). Before God created the world, only God existed. He is eternal, and he made the world as an entity separate from himself and under his control.

Theism also maintains that God is a personal God. In Genesis 1:26 we find him saying, "Let us make man in our image." God speaks here as a person. The question most often asked about this verse is, "To whom does he speak? Who is the 'us' in whose image the man and the woman were created?" Though many have tried to explain away the use of the plural here, we believe that the only problem-free answer is that the plural reflects the plurality of the Godhead, the Trinity.

A third element of biblical theism is that God's will is involved with the world. God expresses his will to his special creatures (the human race). He commanded the man not to eat of "the tree of the knowledge of good and evil" (Gen. 2:16–17). The man and the woman must obey him if they want to continue to enjoy his blessing. God also provided for them everything that is good (note the "it was good" in 1:4, 10, 12, 18, 21, 25, 31). Thus, at an early stage in the biblical narratives, we see that God is good and that he desires the good for his creatures. A central implication of these narratives is, then, that the will of God is the highest good. To find life and blessing, the man and the woman must know God's will. The goodness of God and his will form the basis of much of biblical prophecy. God has a good plan for his world. Prophecy is about that plan.

The biblical view of theism stands in stark opposition to other commonly held nonbiblical views of God. *Deism* is the belief in a creator God who is distinct from the world, but who is not actively involved with the world. Deism has no place for God's personal interaction with the world. The central implication of deism is that the will of man, rather than God, is the highest good. Deism thus results in humanism. A God who is not involved in the world could hardly be behind the glorious visions of biblical prophecy. Deism thus denies that God has a prophetic plan for the ages.

Another view of God not found in the Bible is *pantheism*—the belief that the whole of the material and immaterial world is part of the divine nature. God is the impersonal life force behind all of nature. The eternal being is manifested in the material world. A central implication of pantheism is that there is no ultimate good and evil. All is divine, both the good and evil. It is obvious that the prophetic word, which foresees the ultimate triumph of the good, has no place for pantheism.

The Biblical Idea of Divine Providence

God continues to maintain the world he created (Gen. 8:22). His act of governing the world is called *providence*. Not only does God cause the world to follow its own natural laws, but he also watches over it to ensure that everything goes according to his will and his divine decrees (Eph. 1:11). He makes sure that his eternal decrees are accomplished when, where, and how he intended them.

God's providence is universal—not just over the mighty forces of nature (Neh. 9:6) and the great events of history (2 Chron. 36:23), but over even the smallest natural event and the most insignificant human affair (Luke 12:7). God works in "all things" (Rom. 8:28); nothing is too insignificant to merit his attention and care. He makes the grass grow for cattle (Ps. 104:14) and waters the trees for the birds to nest in (104:16–17). All the animals look to him daily for food (104:27). The very lives of God's creatures depend on the breath God gives them. Were he to stop caring for them, they would die (104:29). He has established and maintains the laws for the ordering of day and night (Jer. 33:20). He also determines the course of human history (Prov. 21:1; Acts 17:26), raising up nations and kingdoms (Dan. 2:37) and bringing them to ruin (2:44).

If God's providential care for his creation is so extensive and pervasive, does anything ever happen by accident? Does anything escape his notice or lie outside his concern? No! When an innocent man, for example, accidentally kills another human being, the Bible says that "God lets it happen" (Ex. 21:13). When men throw dice, "its every decision is from the LORD" (Prov. 16:33). Even things motivated by evil intention can accomplish God's intended good (Gen. 50:20).

Is any room left for human decisions? Are our lives totally predetermined by God? No. We as responsible human beings must plan and control our own lives, though we must not forget God's will (Prov. 16:1). We must "commit to the LORD whatever [we] do" (16:3), in order that our plans may succeed. We must say, "If it is the Lord's will, we will live and do this or that" (James 4:15). In other words, God's providence works through our plans and choices. Human beings always and only do what they will to do. Their will is not coerced by God's will. As Joseph told his brothers, "You intended to harm me, but God intended it for good" (Gen. 50:20). Of their own will, his brothers intended their action for harm, but God intended it for good.

Biblical prophecy is dependent on the idea of divine providence because from the earliest prophecies on, the fulfillment of God's promises was made dependent both on human obedience and divine faithfulness (see Gen. 18:17–19).

Nature

Nature has two meanings, biblically speaking. Strictly speaking, it is that part of God's creation that does not have the freedom to act as it chooses. In a broader sense, however, it is all of creation—everything that exists apart from God himself (including humans and angels). There are several facets to the biblical view of nature.

(1) Nature is the product of God's eternal plan. He planned it and then created it, and now he sustains and governs it. The classic statement of the biblical view of nature comes from the church father Augustine (354–430), who taught that the world is the realization of the mind of God. To be in nature is to be in the mind of God. Augustine does not mean that we are literally inside God's mind, but that everything we see around us as nature—birds, trees, flowers, stones, lakes, rivers, clouds, stars, etc.—was once a mere thought in God's mind. He conceived, planned, and created every detail of what we now know as nature. When we thus walk through nature, we are, as it were, walking through what God planned—just as when we walk through Disneyland, we walk through the plans and thoughts of Walt Disney. Today what we know as Disneyland is the product of his mind, just as nature is the realization of God's mind. It is important to note that Augustine did not invent this biblical concept; he merely articulated it for the first time.

(2) Nature is not a part of God. It was created out of nothing (Gen. 1:1). Apart from the incarnation of Jesus, the second person of the Trinity, God and nature are two distinct entities.

(3) Nature is not eternal. There was a moment when nature came into being (Gen. 1:1), and there will be a moment when it passes away in the coming fire of God's judgment (2 Peter 3:10). In its place will be a "new heavens and a new earth" (Isa. 65:17). This is probably to be understood as a restoration of God's original creation.

(4) God acts in and through nature; he also acts in opposition to nature. Both are miracles. God acted in and through nature when he sent an east wind to divide the waters of the Red Sea in the Exodus (Ex. 14:21); he acted in opposition to nature when he provided the manna for the Israelites (16:4–5).

(5) Nature in itself is good. God created it good (Gen. 1:31), but it is now under his curse (Gen. 3:17b; Rom. 8:19–23). Biblical prophecy is about God's plan to restore his good creation.

(6) Nature is one means of God's revealing himself to humanity (Rom. 1:19–20). There is nothing in nature that reveals God's prophetic plan.

(7) Nature is not free. It follows a course laid out for it by God—a course that is a series of causes and effects (Eccl. 1:4–7). Biblical prophecy is based on the biblical notion that nature, the physical world, is good and plays an important role in God's future plans. The natural world is thus not something that will eventually be done away with. God has an eternal plan for this world.

Biblical and Modern Views of Nature

How does the biblical view of nature compare with the modern view? There are two contending modern views of nature: the scientific view and the New Age view, both of which stand in opposition to the biblical view.

In the modern scientific view of nature, the universe is not considered a creation. The universe has, so to speak, always existed. It is eternal. Moreover, there are no miracles in nature. All activities of nature follow a uniform course of events, operative yet today, from initial causes to their effects. Each event in this web of causes and effects has a cause sufficient to explain it and produces an effect consequent to it. Finally, all activities of nature are morally neutral. According to the modern view, there are no "good" causes and effects and there are no "bad" ones. Progress in nature is the result of the survival of the fittest.

This modern scientific view of nature is a distortion of the biblical view. It is true that all or some of nature is permanent, and that its laws are fixed and unchangeable. According to the Bible, however, nature had a beginning. There is a Creator who brought nature into existence and who will sustain it throughout all eternity. Moreover, the will of the Creator continues to hold sway in his world, determining events and causing miracles. While miracles are not the rule in this world, the Bible teaches that God sometimes uses them to accomplish his purposes. Finally, there is a distinction between good and bad events. Those events and things that bring about God's purposes for creating human beings are good, while those events and things that frustrate God's purposes are evil. In the biblical worldview, God acts according to his will and in accordance with our prayers, while the modern scientific view has little place for either.

Like the scientific view, the modern New Age view of nature teaches that the universe has no Creator above or apart from nature. Rather, it is eternal and possesses an inherent force that makes it essentially divine. That is, the world of nature is a series of manifestations of the divine essence, and human beings are themselves an aspect of the divine being. A tree or animal has equal value to a human being. Since this is so, there are no "good" aspects in nature as opposed to "bad" ones. Seen in its relationship to the whole of nature, all things are equally good.

It is not difficult to see that such a view of nature is inimical to the biblical view. God is apart from nature, and human beings, created in God's image, are the highest good in creation. God's prophetic plan of redemption has human beings primarily in view.

God's Plan of Redemption: The Old Testament

In the midst of God's judgment of the man and the woman immediately after the Fall, he did not leave humanity without hope but gave a word of promise. Though dead in trespasses and sins (Eph. 2:1–3), God did not abandon them to find their own way back to him. Rather, he promised to send a Redeemer, who would crush the head of the serpent (Gen. 3:15) and thus restore humanity to the relationship with God they enjoyed before the Fall. As the Bible unfolds the content of that promise, we gain a greater understanding of his great plan of redemption—a plan that finds its fulfillment in Jesus Christ.

According to the divine promise, the Redeemer would be the "offspring" of a woman (Gen. 3:15), the offspring of Abraham (12:1–3), the offspring of Judah (49:8–12), and the offspring of David (2 Sam. 7:12–16). He would come from the nation of Israel, God's chosen people (Neh. 9:7), as a king (Num. 24:7, 17), and receive an eternal kingdom from God (1 Chron. 17:14; Isa. 9:7; Dan. 7:13–14). He would rule not only his own people, Israel, but also all the nations (Ps. 2:8). Through him all nations would be blessed (Ps. 72:17). He would establish that kingdom by defeating God's enemies in one last great battle (Ezek. 38:7–23; Dan. 7:26), after which the heavens and earth would be restored to their original state of beauty and perfection (Isa. 65:27). The King, though born a child, would, in fact, be the Mighty God of Israel (9:6).

But wait! There is one more detail in the original promise. The promised offspring of the woman, the one who was to crush the head of the serpent, would himself be fatally wounded. The serpent would "strike the heel" of the promised offspring (Gen. 3:15b). There was a price to be paid for redemption. Someone had to pay the penalty for humanity's sin (2:17), and God promised to provide the sacrifice (22:8, 13–14). At first, God instituted sacrifices of goats and bulls (Lev. 16:13–25), but they were insufficient for the permanent removal of the sins of the people (Ps. 51:16). The promised King would offer himself as a sacrificial lamb (Isa. 53:7). He is God's servant, "pierced for our transgressions . . . crushed for our iniquities" (53:5).

But how could this servant die and yet reign forever on the throne of David? The afflicted Job, himself a suffering servant of God (Job 42:8), foresaw the end of the promise: "I know that my Redeemer lives, and that in the end he will stand upon the earth" (19:25). Job foresaw the resurrection of the Promised One. Likewise, David saw that God would not let his "Holy One see decay" (Ps. 16:10; cf. Acts 2:25–32). Thus God's Servant would "be raised and lifted up and highly exalted" after giving his life as a ransom for all (Isa. 52:13b).

God's Plan of Redemption: The New Testament

The Old Testament messianic promise is fulfilled in the life, death, resurrection, and glorious return of the Lord Jesus Christ. The New Testament writers show that Jesus is the promised King, born in a manger; the promised prophet, rejected by his own people; and the promised high priest, who offered his own body as a sacrifice for humanity's sin.

Jesus was born as a baby into the family of David—legally through Joseph (Matt. 1:6–16) and physically through his mother Mary, herself a descendant of David (Luke 3:23–31). He was an heir to David's throne. But he was also the Son of God. At his birth, the angel Gabriel announced to Mary that "the Holy Spirit will come upon you, and . . . the holy one to be born will be called the Son of God" (1:35). God promised Jesus "the throne of his father David, and he will reign over the house of Jacob forever" (1:32–33).

But Israel, the people of God, rejected their King (Matt. 21:33–42). Hence, the kingdom was "taken away" from them and "given to a people who [would] produce its fruit" (21:43). Three times Jesus predicted his rejection and crucifixion by the Jewish leaders (Mark 8:31; 9:31; 10:33). On the evening of the Passover (John 18:28), he was crucified. He was then buried, and after three days he rose from the dead (Luke 24:6) and ascended into heaven (Acts 1:9).

After his ascension, Jesus sent the Holy Spirit (Acts 2:33) to continue his work among his faithful Jewish followers (2:14–21) and the growing body of Gentiles (10:45). Through Peter, Paul, and other missionaries, the church spread throughout the ancient world, extending as far as Rome (28:30). The church now waits patiently for the Lord's return (1 Cor. 15:50–58).

Jesus will return as a mighty warrior to establish his kingdom (Acts 1:11) at the end of the age "with power and great glory" (Matt. 24:30). He will defeat the forces of evil and, finally, crush the head (Rev. 19:15) of "that ancient serpent called the devil or Satan, who leads the whole world astray" (12:9). When he comes, a great tribulation will break out on earth (chs. 6–18). All who are faithful to Jesus Christ will suffer in that persecution. At the end of seven years, those who have died in the persecution will be raised again to new life. Then the kingdom established by Jesus will reunite God's people, Israel, and Jesus Christ will rule over them as Messiah for a thousand years. At the end of the thousand years there will be a second resurrection and a final judgment. Christ will deliver the kingdom to the Father and he will reign forever (1 Cor. 15:28).

The Kingdom of God in the Old Testament

In the Old Testament, God is acknowledged as "the King" (Isa. 6:5), and his rule is called his "kingdom" (Ps. 145:11–13). The basis of God's rule in the world is grounded both in creation and redemption. As *Creator* of the world, God "established his throne in heaven, and his kingdom rules over all" (103:19). The world itself is God's kingdom (104:1–4). Thus, frequently throughout the Old Testament, God is envisioned as the Sovereign "Lord seated on a throne, high and exalted" (Isa. 6:1). The throne is located in the heavenly temple, from which "the whole earth is [filled with] his glory" (6:3). That heavenly temple provides the pattern for the earthly tabernacle (Ex. 26:30) and temple.

God is also known as King through his great act as *Redeemer*. When he redeemed Israel in the Exodus, "the shout of the King [was] among them" (Num. 23:21). The defeat of the Egyptians and Israel's salvation demonstrated to all the nations that "the LORD will reign for ever and ever" (Ex. 15:18). When God brought Israel into the Promised Land and "planted" them in Jerusalem (15:17), he established his sanctuary as his dwelling place, from which he reigned (15:17–18). Thus, as Redeemer King, the throne of God was located in Jerusalem, the City of Zion, "the holy place where the Most High dwells" (Ps. 46:4), his "resting place for ever and ever" (132:13–14). God's rule in Jerusalem, however, does not exclude his universal reign over all the nations. As the psalmist said, "God is the King of all the earth. . . . God reigns over the nations" (47:7–8).

The idea of God's kingdom centered in Jerusalem was so permanently etched in the Old Testament prophetic texts that in spite of the destruction of Jerusalem, the hope remained intact that God would not abandon his people or his chosen city. The prophet Isaiah foresaw that after Jerusalem fell, the Lord would return to that city and would reign again from there among his people (Isa. 52:7–10; cf. 33:17, 22). During the exilic period, the time when the Israelites were in Babylonian captivity, the prophetic hope of the establishment of God's kingdom grew in scope to include even the former enemies of Israel: "Then the survivors from all the nations that have attacked Jerusalem will go up [to Jerusalem] year after year to worship the King, the LORD Almighty" (Zech. 14:16).

The grandest prophetic vision of God's kingdom in the Old Testament comes from Daniel 7, where the kingdom of God is the kingdom of "the Ancient of Days," representing God's authority and power over "all peoples, nations and men of every language" (v. 14).

The Kingdom of God in the Old Testament and the Messiah

In the Old Testament, the Messiah ("anointed one") is the King of Israel. In one of the earliest messianic promises in the Old Testament, Jacob proclaimed that the right of kingship would "not depart from Judah, nor the ruler's staff from between his feet, until he comes to whom it belongs" (Gen. 49:10). The prophet Balaam foresaw the rise of a King of Israel who would defeat Israel's enemies and establish a kingdom over all the empires of the world (Num. 24:17–24). Balaam drew heavily on the imagery of earlier prophecies in the Pentateuch. The coming king, for example, would "crush the foreheads of Moab, the skulls of all the sons of Sheth" (Num. 24:17). This appears to allude to the earliest promise in the Pentateuch, the promise of the "seed of the woman" who would "crush the head" of the seed of the serpent (Gen. 3:15). Balaam thus identified the "seed of the serpent" with Israel's enemies. His prophecy also drew on the themes of God's promise to Abraham (compare Num. 24:9b with Gen. 12:3).

Later, Hannah prayed that God would send the King that Balaam had spoken about, in order to defeat the enemy and judge the world (1 Sam. 2:10). When David became the king of Judah and later all Israel, many hoped he might be the promised King. Those hopes were dashed by the words of the prophet Nathan; David was only the first in a line of kings from whom the last one, the Messiah, would be born (2 Sam. 7:16). Only one of his descendants would establish an eternal kingdom (7:12–14). As the descendants of David came and went (most of whom were evil in the eyes of God), hope began to wane that God's word would be fulfilled through this house. When the city of Jerusalem was destroyed and the people exiled to Babylon, all hope in the historical fulfillment of the promise to David was lost. How could God send a King if there was no longer a kingdom?

The answer to that question lay in the prophets' renewed vision of the future. God would not only reestablish the people of Israel in the Promised Land; he would also send a King from the house of David to rule over Israel and the nations. The fullest expression of that new vision is Daniel 7:11–14. The messianic Son of Man will receive an eternal kingdom from God and be "given authority, glory and sovereign power; all peoples, nations and men of every language [will worship] him. His dominion is an everlasting dominion that will not pass away, and his kingdom is one that will never be destroyed." Thus, for Daniel, the fulfillment of God's promise to David was an eternal heavenly kingdom that God promised to bring to earth.

Jesus and the Kingdom of God in the New Testament

The New Testament writers saw the fulfillment of Jesus' mission as a continuation of the Old Testament prophetic vision of God's kingdom. In so doing, they were simply following the lead of Jesus himself. At the time of his birth, many in Israel were eagerly awaiting the fulfillment of God's promises. An angel came to a young woman of the house of David to announce the birth of the King (Luke 1:26). When the child was born, the faithful of Israel recognized him as the promised King (2:25–32). Great men from the remotest parts of the world came to acknowledge his birth (Matt. 2:1–2)—just as the prophets had foretold (Ps. 72:10).

In his earthly ministry, Jesus' entire understanding of himself and his ministry was wrapped up in the biblical notion of the kingdom of God. He worked and taught as if the promised kingdom of God were being fulfilled in his day. He began his ministry by proclaiming that the kingdom of God was at hand (Matt. 12:28; Mark 1:14–15). He traveled from village to village, preaching "the good news of the kingdom of God" (Luke 4:43). At the close of his ministry, he was welcomed into Jerusalem as the reigning King (Matt. 21:1–9).

There is a tragic irony, however, to the earthly ministry of Jesus. He came as the messianic King, but Israel rejected him (Matt. 21:42–46); therefore, he said that his kingdom, the one whose arrival he himself had announced, was going to be taken away from them and given to a more worthy nation (21:43). Nevertheless, the hope of the promised kingdom still lay in the future, when the Son of Man would appear in the sky "with power and great glory" (24:30). The New Testament ends on the same positive note with which it began: the messianic King is coming!

How did Jesus and the writers of the New Testament understand the consequences of Israel's rejection of his kingdom? Many suggest that since the messianic kingdom was rejected by his own people (Matt. 12:22–37), the establishment of the kingdom was "postponed" until Christ's future return (Acts 3:19–21). Thus Christ's kingdom is yet to be established, just as the Old Testament prophets foretold (3:21); that kingdom will be the rule of Christ during the Millennium (Rev. 20). After the millennial reign of Christ, the kingdom will be given over to God (1 Cor. 15:28) and the eternal kingdom established (Rev. 21–22). Others view the Jewish rejection of Jesus' offer of the kingdom as the means whereby God's Old Testament kingdom promises were transferred to God's new kingdom, the church. That view, called amillennialism, understands the Old Testament prophecies to apply figuratively, or spiritually, to the church.

The Kingdom of God in Christian Theology

Christian theology has developed the biblical notion of the kingdom of God in two directions. Some understand it in physical, realistic terms. The kingdom of God is a sphere, a realm, over which God rules. In Old Testament times, the kingdom was located in Jerusalem and lasted throughout the Davidic monarchy. Since the New Testament, some identify the kingdom with the church, whose spreading influence is thus the spread of the kingdom. For others, notably those who do not identify the church with the Old Testament kingdom, the realm of the kingdom is taken to be the future reign of Christ in Jerusalem during the Millennium.

Others, however, have understood the concept of the kingdom of God as a spiritual-ethical ideal. The kingdom of God is not so much a place as it is a reign or relationship. It is God's rule in the hearts of believers. When Christians gather together to do the work of God, they advance God's kingdom and spread its influence in the hearts and lives of others. These two views of the kingdom of God have played a crucial role in defining the nature of Christianity throughout the centuries.

In the early centuries of the church, when it was a small, scattered, and struggling group of believers, the concept of the kingdom of God as a future realm yet to be established predominated. Christians looked forward to a future, earthly rule of Christ. As the church began to gain in power and influence, however, the kingdom of God was more and more identified with the realm of the earthly church. Such an earthly identification of the kingdom sparked an equally strong ethical and spiritual reaction. The human soul was viewed as the spiritual Jerusalem, the place where Christ reigned.

In the early medieval church, a partial synthesis of these two views of the kingdom was worked out by Saint Augustine (354–430). He viewed the church on earth as the fulfillment of the earthly millennial reign of Christ, for Christ reigned in the hearts of its members. The spiritual reign of Christ thus was realized in the earthly church. Augustine's view has remained a dominate view of the kingdom of God up to our day, though both the ethical-spiritual and earthly-physical view of the kingdom of God also continue. The ethical-spiritual view has largely secularized its notion of the realm of Christ's kingdom so that it includes social institutions in addition to the church. Modern versions of the "social gospel," for example, often call on governmental agencies to do the work of Christ's kingdom. The earthly-physical view of the kingdom continues in the view of contemporary dispensational evangelicalism. They clearly expect to see the physical establishment of God's kingdom in Jerusalem during the millennial period.

The Biblical Covenants

Throughout the Bible, God established relationships with specific people at specific times by means of covenants. A covenant is a formal agreement between two or more persons, usually involving requirements, promises, and stipulations that had to be kept if the covenant were to remain firm. The covenants were established and maintained by specific procedures.

An agreement between the parties of the covenant could be for a variety of interests. For example, when one entered into a marriage, the marriage bond was usually affirmed by means of a covenant. Covenants were also used in political treaties and international agreements. Boundaries between countries were often agreed upon and marked by means of covenants. In the Bible, God took an accepted social convention, the legal contract, and used it to express his unfailing commitment to humanity and to his chosen people.

The ancient world saw at least two types of covenants or treaties. (1) The "land grant" treaty was used to establish political boundaries. A powerful king parceled out vast territories of his kingdom to loyal tribal chieftains. Each chieftain received a piece of land as a "land grant," with essentially no stipulations attached. There was enough trust in the relationship between the king and his loyal chieftain so that the chieftain could do with it as he pleased. There was, of course, the assumption of the chieftain's loyalty, but that was not specified in the covenant. Hence the treaty was essentially without conditions. (2) The second type of covenant was a "vassal treaty." A powerful king would impose his will on a subordinate king (a vassal), usually one he had defeated in war. The king laid out various stipulations that had to be kept if the terms of the treaty were to be maintained. If the vassal broke the treaty by not keeping its stipulations, severe punishment ensued.

It is common in biblical studies to distinguish between several covenants by means of these two types of ancient treaty forms. The covenant God made with Abraham is usually defined as a form of the "land grant treaty." Without laying down specific stipulations, God simply granted the land of Canaan to Abraham as a promise. God, of course, assumed loyalty on Abraham's part, but no specific terms were spelled out. The covenant God made with Israel at Mount Sinai, however, is like a "vassal treaty." In that covenant, God laid down specific "laws" that the people had to perform as part of the covenant. If they failed to obey those laws, they faced divine punishment. The similarities between these biblical covenants and their ancient Near Eastern counterparts is striking and confirms the basic historicity of the narratives.

The Adamic Covenant

The prophet Hosea specifically refers to God's covenant with Adam in Hosea 6:7, where he mentions Israel's breaking their covenant with God just as Adam had broken his covenant. This reference to the story of Adam and Eve is unusual since there is no explicit mention of such a covenant in Genesis. But we do have a narrative in Genesis that recounts all the formal features of a covenant relationship without using specific covenant terminology. In making his comparison between Israel's sin and Adam's, Hosea was relying on his own careful study of the Genesis narratives and his observation of their covenantal nature.

What was the nature of Adam's covenant? That covenant was grounded in creation. That is, Adam was created within a covenant relationship with God. He was, so to speak, in a covenant relationship with God *by nature*. That relationship was his to enjoy by virtue of his being created in God's image. The will of God he was to obey was written on his heart. Perhaps for those reasons Genesis does not use the word "covenant" to describe Adam's state. Adam did not specifically enter a covenant with God because he already enjoyed such a relationship by virtue of his own creation.

We should also note, however, that God did express his will to Adam in terms of specific stipulations. God said to Adam, "You are free to eat from any tree in the garden" (Gen. 2:16); then he added, "But you must not eat from the tree of the knowledge of good and evil" (2:17a). God then spelled out the consequences of disobedience, "For when you eat of it you will surely die" (2:17b). Though the consequences of obedience are not mentioned, the obvious consequence for Adam and his descendants would have been eternal life. But when they disobeyed God, they were cast out of the Garden of Eden and denied access to the "tree of life" (3:22–24). The implication is that had they obeyed God, they would have continued to enjoy access to the tree of life and hence would have "lived forever" (3:22b).

Genesis 4–5 records how Adam's death—his punishment for disobeying God—was passed on to future generations (cf. Rom. 5:12). In other words, Adam was a kind of representative head for the whole human race. His actions have affected all of us, for we are under the same penalty of death that he suffered. These narratives focus only on what happened and leave us guessing at what that covenant may have meant if Adam and Eve had not sinned. Since sin and rebellion had entered God's world, eternal life was lost and humanity needed salvation. The rest of the Bible is the account of God's restoration of his world and of humanity. That is the central theme of biblical prophecy.

The Noachic Covenant

The first covenant God made with humanity after the Fall was his covenant with Noah (Gen. 9:8–17). That covenant is important to the overall purpose of God because it clearly shows the scope and extent of God's plan of salvation. The Noachic covenant shows that God's plan to restore lost humanity was not focused narrowly on saving human souls. It was rather aimed at the salvation and restoration of all creation. Thus, through the Noachic covenant God entered into a covenant with the whole of creation. This covenant serves as the foundation, the basis, of all subsequent covenants. In essence, the remaining covenants in the Bible are aimed at fulfilling God's sweeping covenant that he established with Noah.

The Noachic covenant began with an offering that Noah presented to God after the Flood. In thanksgiving for God's gracious deliverance, "Noah built an altar to the LORD and . . . sacrificed burnt offerings on it" (Gen. 8:20). God accepted that sacrifice and was moved to promise never again to "curse the ground because of man. . . . And never again will I destroy all living creatures." (8:21). Thereupon God restored creation to its orderly processes (8:22–9:7) and entered the covenant with Noah (9:8–17).

Noah's covenant with God was thus grounded in a sacrifice, a shedding of blood, that God graciously accepted. This narrative gives an important theological lesson about God and his relationship to humanity: The need for atonement is woven into the fabric of his world. A sacrifice must be offered, for "without the shedding of blood there is no forgiveness" (Heb. 9:22). The world is governed by a righteous God, and its order depends on meeting the requirements of his standards. Without atonement, without compensation of God's righteousness, there can be no cosmos; there will only be chaos and destruction (such as the Flood).

These early chapters of Genesis thus lay down the ground rules for all the prophetic events that follow. There is a need for atonement, and God's work of redemption means the shedding of innocent blood. Hence all the biblical covenants anticipate and are grounded on the ultimate sacrifice that God offered in sending his own Son, Jesus, to die on the cross and to establish his new covenant promises.

The sign of the covenant that God gave to Noah was a rainbow—a sign that is open for everyone to see. As such it contrasts curiously with the covenantal sign given to Abraham, the sign of circumcision. Whereas Abraham's covenant was with him and his offspring only, God's covenant with Noah was not only with all humanity, but also with all creation.

The Abrahamic Covenant

Hardly a text in Scripture bears a comparable weight of importance to that of Genesis 12:1–3. These verses are the bull's-eye of biblical prophecy. As important as the Noachic covenant is for establishing the outside perimeters of God's plan of salvation, the Abrahamic covenant provides the focus. In it God takes the necessary steps to restore all humanity to himself. He promises to restore his original blessing to all humanity through the physical seed of Abraham: "All peoples on earth will be blessed through you" (12:3). The blessing spoken of here is the blessing for which God created humanity: "Be fruitful and increase in number; fill the earth and subdue it" (1:28).

While we may debate whether God was instructing Adam to "fill the whole earth" or to "fill the whole land" (i.e., the Promised Land) in Genesis 1:28, in the Abrahamic covenant God speaks of a central role to be played by the Promised Land: "To your offspring I will give this land" (Gen. 12:7). God frequently repeats this promise to Abraham and his descendants (e.g., 22:17–18; 26:3–5; 28:13–14). Thus the promise of the land of Canaan becomes an essential part of the Abrahamic covenant. In that land God will restore his blessing to all the world. It is for this reason that the land and Israel's return to the land is so important to biblical prophecy.

After this covenant, God's plan takes on a decidedly personal and nationalistic focus. He begins to work through the nation of Israel. But his plan does not lose its global purpose. God continues to be concerned about the nations, but only in terms of his dealings with the descendants of Abraham. All subsequent covenants that God made with Israel are based on this covenant with Abraham. When God delivered Israel from Egypt, it was because "he remembered his covenant with Abraham" (Ex. 2:24). When God promised Israel a new covenant, it was to "be true to Jacob, and [to] show mercy to Abraham, as [he] pledged on oath to [the] fathers in days long ago" (Mic. 7:20). God's promise remained firm even though Israel disobeyed God.

Considerable debate has centered on the extent to which the Abrahamic covenant still applies to the physical descendants of Abraham. Does it have the same sense today as it did before the coming of Christ? Does the Abrahamic covenant still hold good for Israel, or has the church taken over its promises? Some believe the church is the rightful heir of the Abrahamic covenant; the church is the new "seed of Abraham." Support for that interpretation is found in those New Testament texts that speak of the church's participation in the new covenant promises (see Gal. 3:29). Others argue that the church only shares in the blessings of the new covenant; it does not take the place of Israel, the physical seed of Abraham. God still intends to keep his promise to Abraham's seed, and they will yet inherit the Promised Land.

The Mosaic Covenant

When God delivered Israel from Egypt, he brought them first to Mount Sinai. There he entered into a covenant with them (Ex. 19:1–9). This was the Mosaic covenant, in which God promised to bless Israel, live with them, and give them the land promised to Abraham. The Mosaic covenant was, in fact, the means by which God intended to fulfill his promises to Abraham (2:24), provided the people obeyed God, kept his commandments, and put their trust solely in him. God would give them victory over their enemies, and Israel would be a light to the nations in their land. Through their obedience, God's will would be revealed to all (Deut. 4:1–8).

Almost from the start, Israel failed to obey the covenant. Even while God was warning Moses on Mount Sinai of the dangers of idolatry (Ex. 20:1–6), the people and their leaders were melting their jewelry and fashioning the idolatrous golden calf (32:1–6). God's response to Israel's disobedience was to give them more laws, which governed every detail of their lives and were intended to safeguard them from falling away into idolatry. According to the apostle Paul, these laws were given to Israel because of their transgressions (Gal. 3:19), to keep Israel from straying too far from God until the Messiah came (3:21–25).

The laws of the Mosaic covenant begin with the Ten Commandments (Ex. 20:1–7) and a set of forty-two laws called "The Covenant Code" (20:22–23:19). These laws lay down the general principles on which Israel's relationship with God was to be governed. Then follows a large collection of laws that regulate the work of the priests (Ex. 25–Lev. 16) and the lives of the lay people (Lev. 17–26). The book of Deuteronomy summarizes all these laws.

In spite of Israel's failure, God remained faithful to Abraham and did not cast off his people Israel. His covenant at Sinai remained firm (Ex. 34:10). He was "the compassionate and gracious God, slow to anger, abounding in love and faithfulness, maintaining love to thousands, and forgiving wickedness, rebellion and sin" (34:6–7). When Israel refused to believe in God in the desert (Num. 14:11), God raised up a another generation and brought them into the land. When they also proved faithless (Judg. 2:10–12), God sent judges to deliver them from their enemies and to lead them in the way of the Lord (2:16–18). He "had compassion on them as they groaned under those who oppressed and afflicted them" (2:18b). Ultimately their unbelief led to their exile into another land (2 Kings 17:14; 25:1–26).

The Mosaic covenant ended with Israel's failure, but God's faithfulness endured, for there was hope beyond the Exile (Lam. 4:22). That hope was not grounded in the Mosaic covenant, but in God's promises to the house of David (the Davidic covenant) and the new covenant.

The Davidic Covenant

The Davidic covenant has a central place in Scripture. It is the foundation for most of the messianic prophecies in the Old Testament; it is the historical means by which God fulfilled his promises to Abraham; and it is the basis on which the New Testament's view of the future kingdom of God is built.

The Davidic covenant was promised to David late in his life, when he had firmly established his kingdom over Israel (2 Sam. 7:1). David wanted to build a palace for himself and a temple for God. God permitted him to built the former but not the latter. Someone else would build a temple in Jerusalem. That "someone" became the central focus of the Davidic covenant (7:8–16). In it, God promised to make David's kingdom an eternal kingdom and to give David's house (i.e., his dynasty) an eternal ruler. That ruler was to be one of David's sons (7:12). The sign of his coming would be the building of the temple in Jerusalem (7:13). The Lord promised David, "Your house and your kingdom will endure forever before me; your throne will be established forever" (7:16).

We are first led to believe that God's promise to David was fulfilled in the reign of Solomon. Within the narrative, Solomon himself believed he was the son whom God promised David, for he set about building the temple (see 1 Kings 5:5). But the Lord's reply to Solomon presented the following warning: "As for this temple you are building, if you follow my decrees, carry out my regulations and keep all my commands and obey them, I will fulfill through you the promise I gave to David" (6:12). Now, that's a big "if"— an "if" that neither he nor any of the historical Davidic kings who followed him were able to accomplish. In fact, on this very basis Scripture disqualified every historical king who reigned in Jerusalem and Israel's leaders after the Exile. Even when the hope of the fulfillment of the Davidic covenant began to build around the high priest Joshua after the Exile (Zech. 6:9–13), the prophet Zechariah warned Israel: "This will happen if you diligently obey the LORD your God" (6:15).

In other words, the Old Testament closes on the note that no Davidic king had ever come who could claim to be the fulfillment of God's promise to David. That promise remained open until the coming of Jesus Christ. The angel Gabriel told Mary when he announced the birth of Jesus, "The Lord God will give him the throne of his father David, and he will reign over the house of Jacob forever; his kingdom will never end" (Luke 1:32–33). Jesus was the promised son of David. He came to announce the kingdom of God, and he is coming again to establish it here on earth.

The New Covenant

Along with the Davidic covenant, the new covenant receives a central focus in biblical prophecy. Though the name "new covenant" comes from Jeremiah 31:31, God's promise of it is already found in the Pentateuch (e.g., Deut. 30:1–14). In fact, one of the central themes of the Pentateuch, and most of the Old Testament, is the promise of the new covenant.

What is the new covenant? There are essentially two different answers—the difference lies in how one understands the word "new." (1) Some understand it to be a "renewing" of the Mosaic covenant (see "Covenant Theology" in the Glossary). The new covenant, in other words, is a different version of the Mosaic covenant, in which God gave Israel his laws on tablets of stone. In the new covenant, those laws are written on their hearts. Note Jeremiah 31:33: "This is the covenant I will make with the house of Israel. . . . I will put my law in their minds and write it on their hearts." What is new about the new covenant, then, is that the law that God gave Israel at Sinai is to be internalized—written on their hearts.

(2) Others, however, view the new covenant as more distinct. They understand the word "new" to mean something new and different from the Mosaic covenant. Israel could not keep the Mosaic covenant, so God gave them a new covenant. Support for this view comes also from Jeremiah. The Lord says, for example, that the new covenant "will not be like the covenant I made with their forefathers when I took them by the hand to lead them out of Egypt, because they broke my covenant" (Jer. 31:32). The Mosaic covenant required obedience to the specific stipulations given to Moses at Sinai; the new covenant will require a life transformed by the power of God's Spirit. "I will give you a new heart and put a new spirit in you. . . . I will put my Spirit in you and move you to follow my decrees and be careful to keep my laws" (Ezek. 36:26–27). In these passages, the newness of the new covenant seems to be more than a renewal of the Mosaic covenant. It is a new kind of covenant (see Heb. 8:12).

For whom is the new covenant given? Who will enjoy its blessings today or in the future? In the Old Testament contexts that refer to the new covenant, it is promised to the people of Israel (e.g., Jer. 31:31). If that covenant is yet to be fulfilled, then God has a future plan for Israel. On the other hand, the New Testament contains passages that suggest its blessings have already been inherited by the church (e.g., Heb. 9:15). Dispensationalists generally believe that, though the church may now enjoy the blessings of the new covenant (such as the gift of the Holy Spirit), it is with Israel alone that it will one day in the future be fulfilled. Covenant theology believes that the new covenant promises are now fulfilled in the church, the new Israel.

Prophecy in the Old Testament

The Big Picture

It is important to start by looking at the "big picture" of Old Testament prophecy. It is easy to miss the forest for the trees. It is, in fact, easy to miss the trees themselves in the Old Testament. Some of the most important books of the Old Testament are so massive and complicated that it is hard to see the whole tree at once (e.g., the Torah of Moses [Pentateuch], or the book of Isaiah or Ezekiel). Sometimes all we can see is the trunk or the bark.

A helpful way to start is by viewing the Old Testament as Jesus and the Jews in his day saw it. By the time of Christ, the Jews were reading all Scripture as a single unit, and each part fit together into the whole. The shape they gave to the Scriptures consisted of a threefold division, "the Law, the Prophets, and the Writings." Jesus himself referred to this division "the Law of Moses, the Prophets and the Psalms [the first book of the Writings]" (Luke 24:44).

Not only did the Scriptures have a definite shape, but that shape reflected the sense or meaning that was understood to be at the heart of the Old Testament. Many scholars today recognize that this threefold shape was used in order to show that these Scriptures were to be read as prophecies of the coming Messiah. Jesus himself indicated that in the threefold division, "everything must be fulfilled that is written about me" (Luke 24:44). Though we could say much at this point, suffice it to say that the Old Testament Scriptures have a definite shape and that behind that shape lies an understanding that these texts are fundamentally messianic.

Who gave the Old Testament its shape? Who were its final editors? According to tradition, it was Ezra the scribe (see Ezra 7:10). According to the NIV, this verse reads, "For Ezra had devoted himself to the study and observance of the Law of the LORD and to teaching its decrees and laws in Israel." Let me suggest, however, another translation: "For Ezra had devoted himself to the study of the Torah of the LORD and to composing it in order to teach Israel its central meaning." Whether or not it was Ezra who gave us the final version of the Old Testament Scriptures, we can say with confidence that it was someone who knew God's Word and who was intent on teaching its central focus. That central focus was God's plan to bring salvation to Israel and redemption to the world.

For the most part, the early Jewish readers of the Old Testament understood the whole of the Old Testament to be a prophecy of, and for, their own future. Consequently, all the biblical authors were understood to have been prophets (cf. Dan. 9:10).

The Shaping of the Old Testament

We know that the entire Old Testament received its present shape sometime after the Exile (i.e., after 539 B.C.). That time, it turns out, was a crucial period in the history of Israel. It was a time of severe testing for God's people, a time when Israel's hopes and faith in God's promises had all but been dashed to pieces, a time when it seemed as if all God's promises had not only not come about, but were less likely than ever to be fulfilled. During this time Daniel, in captivity in Babylon, wondered why the prophetic words had not yet been fulfilled (Dan. 9:1–2). He had understood from reading Jeremiah that the Messiah and his kingdom would come at the close of the Babylonian Captivity. But that time had come, and there was still no Messiah. Daniel could not understand what went wrong. Thus he searched the words of Jeremiah (Jer. 25:11) and sought the Lord's help in understanding them.

God answered Daniel's prayer. He sent the angel Gabriel to reveal to him the precise time of the coming of the Messiah. The Messiah would not be coming after the seventy years of captivity, because (as Daniel's prayer in ch. 9 shows) Israel had not remained faithful to God's covenant (Mosaic covenant). Israel was still not ready for the coming of the Messiah. His coming would be delayed until their transgression was complete and their wickedness atoned (Dan. 9:24). That would not happen until after sixty-nine "weeks" of years (9:25–26)—that is, 483 years. Though it is not a simple matter of calculation, the traditional reckoning of years from Daniel's day to the coming of Jesus fits comfortably within that time frame.

The Old Testament Scriptures were thus collected and shaped during one of the darkest hours of Israel's history. The people were in great need of renewed hope in the promises of God. For their first readers, the prophetic Scriptures were, as Peter said, "a lamp shining in a dark place" (2 Peter 1:19). Those who gathered and formed the various books of the Old Testament into the single collection we now possess were themselves eagerly awaiting the coming of the Messiah. They read the Scriptures with that hope in mind, and their expectation is reflected in their work. They saw those themes inherent in the books they were shaping and provided the reader with an appropriate context for understanding their messianic sense. Thus the shape they gave to the final form of the Old Testament was, in effect, a reading sequence that enabled one to see more clearly the prophetic picture of the Messiah.

The Composition
of the Individual Books of the Old Testament

If we direct our attention away from the Old Testament Scriptures as a whole and focus on the individual books, we see there too that the shape of each book reflects a deep interest in Israel's messianic and prophetic hope. The final editors of the Old Testament were not the only ones who cast their texts in a messianic mold. The biblical authors themselves worked hard at arranging and refining individual texts into a final and complete picture that reflects their intent and meaning.

A prophetic book of great importance is the book of Isaiah. This book contains both the words of Isaiah and a narrative story about the prophet. Its purpose is to present to its readers the message of the prophet during some of the darkest days of Israel's apostasy, when Israel, God's people, were being sorely oppressed by the cruel and mighty Assyrian empire. In that context Isaiah offered not only threats of judgment and divine wrath, but also words of comfort and hope—God would send a Redeemer (Isa. 7:14; 9:6) and establish his kingdom (chs. 11–12). This Redeemer would be a king who would arise from the house of David (Isa. 9:7).

Early in the book readers are given the intial impression that the Redeemer will come in Isaiah's own day. However, after chapters 36–39, the prophet begins to focus his attention beyond the time of Israel's oppression under Assyria and the time of their exile into Babylon. The second half of this book actually looks to the time of the return from Exile. In so doing, it raises the question whether Isaiah's visions were to be fulfilled during the days of Israel's return from Babylon or whether they, like Daniel, point far beyond those days. Do Isaiah's words point to the time of Jesus?

As we keep reading Isaiah, we quickly see that the prophet's visions point beyond both the immediate events of his own day and the days of Israel's return from captivity. His visions point to the future days of the coming Messiah, the Servant of the Lord, who would suffer for his own people and for the nations and would usher in a time of peace and prosperity (Isa. 53). Ultimately, we learn that these visions extend into a future that includes "new heavens and a new earth" (65:17) and an eternal peace for the people of God. This raises the question of whether Isaiah's words also look beyond the first coming of Christ to his second coming. That is, in fact, how they are understood in the New Testament.

What is true of Isaiah is true for the rest of the books of the Old Testament. Each one is composed with an overriding purpose—to announce the coming of the Messiah and the fulfillment of God's eternal plans.

The Individual Words of Prophecy

The prophetic books contain numerous abstracts of the words of the prophets—words they spoke on specific public occasion and words that were edited and preserved as Scripture. It is something like a radio program that uses the recorded messages of a well-known preacher. Those messages are edited and shaped to fit a half-hour format.

What do these prophetic words say about Christ and the future? It is easy to read the Old Testament and come away thinking these books are only about God's specific dealings with the people of Israel in the past. But their purpose was not merely to inform us of those events. They reveal God's eternal plan as it played out in Israel's past. The past was the divine canvas on which God painted his plans for the future. The prophetic word is full of pictures that teach its readers about God's plans and purposes for Israel's future.

This fact places a great deal of responsibility on us, the readers of these texts. We must not only read them but also understand what the writers of these books were getting at. I remember well the old Steve Allen Show. Someone once asked Steve Allen, "Do they get your show in Nebraska?" He answered them, "Well, it goes there, but I'm not sure they get it." Understanding the prophetic word is a lot like that. We can often understand the words, but sometimes we just don't get the message.

We may take some comfort in the fact that many times the prophets themselves did not fully understand the "big picture." Note Peter's words in 1 Peter 1:10–12:

> Concerning this salvation, the prophets, who spoke of the grace that was to come to you, searched intently and with the greatest care, trying to find out the time and circumstances to which the Spirit of Christ in them was pointing when he predicted the sufferings of Christ and the glories that would follow. It was revealed to them that they were not serving themselves but you, when they spoke of the things that have now been told you by those who have preached the gospel to you by the Holy Spirit sent from heaven.

Since prophecy is so difficult to understand, we must look again to the instruction in 2 Peter 1:20, which tells us that each prophetic word must not only be understood within its own context but also within the larger prophetic picture in Scripture. Note also the advice for understanding prophecy in Hosea 14:9, where the prophet tells his readers that the only ones who are going to "get" his meaning are those who already have wisdom and understanding! Some will stumble at his words, but the wise and discerning "will understand them."

Prophetic Snapshots

To understand the words of the prophets one must be able to recognize the verbal pictures they give. The whole range of Old Testament prophecy is, in fact, an array of "word pictures." When read together, these pictures give us a composite view of God's great plan for the ages. The use and reuse of these pictures is consistent throughout Scriptures. Learning to identify them helps one see what the prophets were getting at in their otherwise compact and formidable way of speaking. The following is a brief list of some key prophetic pictures.

(1) *Living in Paradise: God's gift of the Promised Land.* The prophets repeatedly turn to God's original purpose for the human race. Nowhere is that view portrayed with such clarity and simplicity as in Genesis 1–2. There, in God's world and God's garden, humanity was to enjoy God's good gift of the land. There they were to enjoy God's fellowship. And there they were to worship and serve their Creator forever. Though humanity lost this Paradise through the Fall, God's plan was to restore it. This picture remains at the center of the prophetic hope and finds it ultimate fulfillment in Revelation 21–22.

(2) *Paradise lost: The fall of Satan and humanity.* The Bible clearly affirms that evil now exists in God's good world. That evil came from a single rebellious act of a one-time great angel, Lucifer. Jesus calls him "a liar" (John 8:44), and the book of Revelation identifies him as "that ancient serpent called the devil or Satan, who leads the whole world astray" (Rev. 12:9). Both views of Satan allude to the picture of the Fall in Genesis 3. The Bible also teaches that the human race has fallen from its original state or righteousness. Humanity not only lost that righteousness, but also gained a corrupt, fallen nature. They need a Redeemer.

(3) *Paradise regained: The return to the Garden of Eden.* All biblical prophecy is about the return to Paradise, the Garden of Eden. Almost all human cultures have mythical literature about a "lost Paradise" and a striving to "return to Paradise." The Bible thus speaks to a basic and universal need of humanity. It is not that the Bible merely gives another version of the "golden age" ideal. Rather, the Bible is the true version of what humanity has always longed for in its myths. Among the many facets to the biblical idea of a return to Paradise, the central elements are: (a) the last battle; (b) the slain Victor; and (c) resurrection and restoration. All three themes find their first statement in Genesis 3 and are subsequently woven into the fabric of most of Old and New Testament visions of the future.

Living in Paradise:
God Created the Universe and the Land

We begin our look at "prophetic snapshots" with a real masterpiece—
the creation account in Genesis 1 and 2. The Genesis account unfolds in three
stages. The first stage is God's work of creating the universe: "In the beginning God created the heavens and the earth" (1:1). God created the whole universe that we see around us today. But if the whole of the universe was created in this first verse, then what is the rest of the chapter about? Were not
the sun, moon, and stars created on the fourth day? How could there be a
universe in verse 1 without the sun, moon, and stars, which appear to be created in verses 14–16?

Throughout most of the history of the church, the common solution to
this problem was that the universe created in verse 1 consisted only of the "raw
material," from which God then made the parts (e.g., the sun, moon, and stars).
God made a "formless" mass "in the beginning" and later used it to make
the world as we know it. This view was largely abandoned a little over a hundred years ago in favor of the "gap theory." According to this theory, God
made the whole universe in the first verse (Gen. 1:1), but it was subsequently
destroyed when Satan fell and thus had to be re-created. That "re-creation"
is recorded in the rest of Genesis 1. The problem with the gap theory is that
there is no compelling evidence of a "gap" of time between verses 1 and 2.

There is, however, another way of looking at the creation account in Genesis 1—one that solves the problem we have raised. It is a view that the prophet
Jeremiah held regarding the focus of this passage. God sent Jeremiah to proclaim his judgment against the nations who lived in and near the Promised Land.
His message was clear and straightforward: These nations had sinned against
God and were thus in danger of divine judgment. That judgment would con-
sist of God's taking their land away and giving it to the Babylonian king, Nebuchadnezzar. God told Jeremiah to say to these people, "With my great power
and outstretched arm I made the earth [land] and its people and the animals
that are on it, and I give it to anyone I please" (Jer. 27:5). God then continues,
"Now I will hand all your countries over to my servant Nebuchadnezzar king of
Babylon" (27:6). The implication of this text is clear. Jeremiah is alluding to the
creation account in Genesis 1, which he understood as an account of the creation
of the Promised Land. In the words he chooses, Jeremiah is not referring to Genesis 1:1, but to the account of creation in 1:2–2:25, in which God prepared the
Promised Land. Thus God created the universe (1:1), and then God made the
Promised Land as a place for humanity to live. Already at the beginning of God's
work of creation, then, the Bible's focus is on the Promised Land. The future
of Israel and all the nations lies in the redemption and restoration of that land.

Questions About the Interpretation of Genesis 1

We cannot do justice to the interpretation of Genesis 1. We will thus attempt to address a few important questions raised by the previous discussion.

(1) *When did God create the universe?* There are three words in Hebrew that mean "beginning": one means "a beginning point in time"; another means "the first of a series" (as in "the first day of the week"); the third means "the initial segment of something" (see Gen. 10:10 RSV, where the cities of Babel, Erech, and Accad are called the "beginning of [Nimrod's] kingdom"; presumably this took some time to accomplish). The word "beginning" in Genesis 1:1 has the last meaning. It means "the first part of something," or "a beginning that is a duration of time." Thus, in Hebrew, Genesis 1:1 does not say God created the universe in the first micro-second of time. It says that God created the universe over some duration of time. We might well translate it: "During the beginning, God created the heavens and the earth."

(2) *How long was that initial duration during which God created the universe?* We cannot say. The Hebrew word "beginning" allows for any length of time; it may have been millions or billions of years. What is important, however, is that in the rest of the chapter, the time frame is limited to the creation of the Promised Land and human beings. The land was covered with water, and there were no fruit trees and animals there. God thus prepared the land during a six-day week, and on the sixth day of that week he created the man and woman.

(3) *What about the creation of light?* When God says in verse 3, "Let there be light," this does not imply that he is here creating light for the first time. The word "light" here refers to sunlight and presupposes God had already created the sun. When God said, "Let there be light," he was simply marking the beginning of this week with the sunrise. The land is covered with darkness because it was nighttime. Note the conclusion of this day: "and there was evening, and there was morning." The author calls the darkness with which this day began "evening."

(4) *Is the creation of the sun, moon, and stars recorded in Genesis 1:14–16?* If these heavenly bodies were created in verse 1, then what is being described in verses 14–16? Most English translations of verse 14 read, "Let there be lights in the expanse of the sky to separate the day from the night." In the Hebrew text, however, God says, "Let the lights in the expanse of the sky be for separating the day from the night." In other words, God is simply declaring that the sun, moon, and stars will divide day from night. The Hebrew text assumes that the sun, moon, and stars have already been created, as in verse 1.

Living in Paradise:
God Created the Promised Land

The account of God's preparation of the Promised Land in Genesis 1 is carefully linked with the similar account of the creation of the Garden of Eden in chapter 2. Not only are the two accounts parallel; they are also similar. In chapter 1, for example, the waters form the boundaries for the dry land that God prepared, just as in chapter 2 the waters form the boundaries for the Garden of Eden. In chapter 1 God plants fruit trees to nourish the man and woman, just as in chapter 2 he plants a garden of fruit trees for nourishment (note that only fruit trees are spoken of). In both chapters 1 and 2 the animals accompany the man and the woman in the land. Such parallels have long led readers of the Bible to suggest that the subject matter of the two chapters is the same divine act—God's creation or preparation of the Garden of Eden, the Promised Land. Chapter 2 is a "close-up" version of chapter 1 and provides explanations of key parts.

The focus on the land where the man and the woman are to dwell is on a "good land," filled with God's gracious provisions. It is, in fact, just like the land promised to Israel, "a good land—a land with streams and pools of water ... with wheat and barley, vines and fig trees, pomegranates, olive oil and honey; a land where bread will not be scarce and you will lack nothing" (Deut. 8:7–9). This is the "good land" that Israel lost through their disobedience, but which is still promised to them in God's covenants. God promised Abraham, "To your descendants I give this land, from the river of Egypt to the great river, the Euphrates" (Gen. 15:18). These are the same boundaries as the Garden of Eden in Genesis 2. In the prophetic vision of the future messianic kingdom, the Promised Land is identified with the Garden of Eden (Isa. 51:3; Ezek. 36:35); the new Jerusalem is a restored Garden of Eden (Rev. 21:1–22:5).

These two chapters also emphasize the animals that accompany the man and the woman in the land. The scene presented is of a close harmony among all God's creatures. The man and woman dwell together in God's good land at peace with the rest of creation. Fruit trees have been provided to nourish the man and woman. This picture plays a key role throughout most of the later biblical prophecies. Isaiah, for example, stresses the future harmony among God's creatures (Isa. 65:25) as well as God's provision of vineyards and fruit trees (65:21–22) in the future promised land (65:25b). Prophetic texts also frequently refer to taming and subduing the "beasts" (Dan. 7; Rev. 19:19–21).

Living in Paradise: Worship

Genesis 2 is a comprehensive explanation of what it means to be created in God's image (1:26–27). Humanity's creation in God's image entails two basic purposes for their existence: fellowship and worship.

(1) *Fellowship*. Fellowship, both with God and with the rest of humanity, is already suggested in Genesis 1:26, where God says, "Let *us* make man in *our* image, in *our* likeness." The plurality of the Godhead provides the model for human beings in fellowship. Creation in God's image means not only that fellowship with God is possible, but also fellowship with other human beings. That fellowship, vertically with God and horizontally with other human beings, is the basis of much of the Old Testament's prophetic view of God's purpose and plan for creation.

That point is illustrated in Genesis 2. When God fashioned the various animals and brought them to Adam to name, he watched closely to see what Adam would name each one. He was watching for a recognition on Adam's part of a true companion—one like himself, and thus also like God. God did not want him to be without company or companionship. But after the animals had all been named, Adam still had not found a "suitable" companion for a human being (2:20b). When God then made another human being and brought her to the man, Adam said in effect, "At last! Here is one like myself!" and he named her accordingly (2:23).

(2) *Worship*. When God created the man and woman, he had already prepared a place where they could meet for fellowship and worship—the Garden of Eden. Much of the description of this garden parallels the description of the tabernacle (and later the temple). The purpose of the tabernacle was to provide a place for worship and fellowship with God, just like the Garden.

In Genesis 2:15 the Hebrew text says that God "rested" the man in the Garden. God rested on the Sabbath and also rested the man. Furthermore, God placed the man in the Garden for worship and obedience (the usual translations "to work it and take of it" are better rendered "to worship and obey"). Such a view of God's purpose for the human race fits well in the larger picture of the Torah. When God made his covenant with Israel on Mount Sinai, his goal was that Israel should be a "kingdom of priests." This is precisely the view of God's purpose that lies at the heart of the prophetic view of the future. Just as humanity was created to have fellowship with God and to worship him forever, God's plan of the ages is to restore that original purpose. At the close of the Bible, when Christ establishes his kingdom on earth, the goal of all believers will again be that of worshiping God as priests: "they will be priests of God and of Christ and will reign with him for a thousand years" (Rev. 20:6).

Paradise Lost: The Fall of Satan

Satan and demons play a central role in the prophetic view of the future. Evil exists in God's good world, but it is not eternal. God will one day destroy Satan and remove his evil influence from his good creation. Evil came from a single rebellious act of a one-time great angel of God, Lucifer. In Jude 6 we are told that some angels "did not keep their positions of authority but abandoned their own home." From several passages we can reconstruct a general outline of what the Bible teaches about Satan and his demons.

Satan and his demons are clearly fallen angels. They were created good along with the rest of God's creation, but they later rebelled and lost their standing with God and became God's eternal enemies. The Bible calls them "spiritual forces of evil in the heavenly realms" (Eph. 6:12). Through them sin and rebellion entered into the human race and the rest of creation (see Genesis 3). The serpent who tempted Eve in the Garden of Eden was Satan. The very word "Satan," in fact, means "adversary."

We learn more about the fall of Satan in the prophetic imagery Ezekiel uses to describe the forces of evil in his own day. Ezekiel accuses the king of Tyre of the same sin of pride and arrogance that the angel Lucifer (Satan) displayed in his defiant rebellion from God's rule. Thus, by paying close attention to Ezekiel's imagery (Ezek. 28:11–19), we can catch a glimpse of the events that led to Satan's fall. Originally, Satan was "the model of perfection, full of wisdom and perfect in beauty" (28:12). He lived "in Eden, the garden of God" (28:13), surrounded by the beauty prepared for him when he was created (28:13). He was "blameless in [his] ways" (28:15). All this changed, however, when his "heart became proud on account of [his] beauty" (28:17) and his wisdom was corrupted (28:17).

Isaiah uses similar imagery as he describes the fall of Babylon (Isa. 14:3–23); through it we can add to our picture of the fall of Satan. Satan is the "morning star" (Lucifer), "fallen from heaven" (14:12). He said in his heart, "I will ascend to heaven; I will raise my throne above the stars of God; I will sit enthroned on the mount of assembly. . . . I will make myself like the Most High" (14:13–14). In other words, pride and power lay at the heart of his sin. It is thus no accident that Satan's first temptation of Eve centered on her desire to "be like God" (Gen. 3:5).

The biblical writers take seriously the threat of Satan and his angels. They pose the central threat to God's kingdom. Their end, however, is sealed (Rev. 20:7–10).

Paradise Lost: Humanity's Fall

The human race has fallen from its original state and is in need of a Redeemer. Much of the prophetic view of the future is centered on the Redeemer. The account of the Fall in Genesis 3 treats the problem of evil and temptation, though the author does not openly reflect on what transpired. We are given little help from the author in understanding the events we are reading. We, the readers, must make sense of the story to answer the questions it raises. We must seek our clues to the story's meaning from the few signs that it and other Scriptures contain.

What, then, does this story teach us about the Fall? (1) The act that precipitated the Fall was a transgression of God's will. God had simply told the man and the woman not to eat of the tree (Gen. 2:16–17), but they disobeyed. That act led to horrendous consequences. (2) The man and the woman were cast off from God's presence and barred from access to the Tree of Life. This means they began to experience both spiritual and physical death. (3) They were immediately aware, in their nakedness, of the shame and guilt of their sin. Their attempt to cover their own nakedness is a picture of all subsequent human attempts to cover sin and its effects. (4) In their one act of disobedience, "sin entered the world . . . and death through sin" (Rom. 5:12; cf. v. 17); "the judgment followed one sin and brought condemnation" (5:16; cf. v. 18). (5) God was not the author of sin. He permitted the Fall, but it was the man and woman, of their own volition, who transgressed God's command. In that regard, the serpent played an important role in the story. His presence shows that it was not God who tempted the first couple to sin. It was the serpent, as an instrument of Satan (Rev. 12:9).

How could the man and woman, created just and good, succumb to temptation and sin? It was not because they had been created with an evil inclination. They were created with the ability not to sin, but they were caught in the trap of wanting more than they had. They became greedy, wanting to be like God and wanting to control their own destiny by obtaining the knowledge of good and evil. They were no longer willing to trust God. Now it was impossible for them not to sin. They were depraved, and that depravity was passed on to all subsequent generations (Gen. 6:5). This is what is called "original sin." David says, for example, "Surely I was sinful at birth, sinful from the time my mother conceived me" (Ps. 51:5). Original sin is that corrupt disposition of the heart by which we are unable to do good and are prone to do evil.

The prophetic texts are grounded in the need for redemption and focus on the divine plan to accomplish it. It is interesting to note that in Genesis, the account of the Fall finds its conclusion in the building of the city of Babylon. Babylon thus became a central theme in Bible prophecy. Babylon, for the prophets, is a dramatic picture of humanity's rebellion against God and his plan of redemption.

Paradise Regained:
The Return to the Garden of Eden

Our look at the "prophetic snapshots" that make up the total picture of God's plan of the ages has now led us to the "Return to the Garden of Eden." The concept of a "return" can best be seen within the larger prophetic framework noted in the chart below:

Creation	Exile	Eschaton ("Last Days")
The Land (Paradise)	Land Lost (Paradise Lost)	Land Regained (Paradise Regained)

A basic pattern is reflected in the concept of a "return." (1) It begins with the notion of a "homeland," a place where one belongs. Man and woman were meant to live in the Promised Land (i.e., Paradise). They are created from the very soil of the land itself. They belong there by virtue of God's gracious provision. They can continue to live there and enjoy God's gifts if they obey his commandments.

(2) The man and the woman were disobedient and were thus cast out of their land (Gen. 3:23). Paradise was lost. In terms of the larger biblical picture, the man and the woman are cast as exiles from the land. This banishment from Paradise and Israel's later experience of the Exile into Babylon are thus two parallel themes that repeatedly occur in biblical prophecy. The prophet Joel, for example, pictured Israel's exile from the land as a great fire that devoured their land and left them homeless. When the enemy's army swooped down on the land like a plague of locusts, he said, "Before them the land is like the garden of Eden, behind them, a desert waste" (Joel 2:3).

(3) It is within that literary and thematic context that the prophetic notion of the "return from exile" is to be understood. That return is more than merely being released from prison, more than an exodus; it is a retaking of the land. All of Israel's fortunes are restored. They are truly home again, present with God and trusting in his grace. Thus Isaiah's vision of Israel's return from Babylon pictures them as renewed in strength, running vigorously without becoming weary (Isa. 40:30–31). They are like Job, who received double from the Lord for all his losses (Job 42:12–17). The writer literally says of Job that "the LORD restored *his captivity*" (42:10). The return from exile thus becomes a thematic picture of God's future blessing for his faithful remnant. When therefore the prophets speak of the "return," they are talking about the establishment of the coming messianic kingdom, not merely an historical event from the past.

Paradise Regained: The Last Battle (Part 1)

The first hint of a final conflict, a last battle, in the Bible is Genesis 3:15a. In his judgment on the serpent, the Lord said, "I will put enmity between you and the woman, and between your offspring and hers; he will crush your head, and you will strike his heel." Thus, already in the Garden of Eden, the Lord begins to speak of the last battle.

The poetic imagery of this passage has led to more than one interpretation. Some see only a reference to the perennial struggle between humans and snakes. Such a view, however, can hardly be the one that the biblical author intends. For him the events he is recording here are clearly of fundamental importance. He understands the grave consequences of Adam and Eve's deed, that they portend of the final destiny of the human race. Thus, when viewed within the larger context of the Pentateuch, God's words to the serpent (who represents Satan; see Rev. 12:9) should be read as God's final verdict on the devil. That does not mean the text has no ambiguities. It is, in fact, deliberately "open." It intends only to put the reader on alert. It intends to raise questions, not answer them: Who is the offspring of the woman? Whose head is to be crushed? Only further reading in the Scriptures can answer these questions.

A further word about the future of the "offspring" ("seed") of the woman is given in Genesis 9:25–27. At first this passage seems insignificant and obscure. It is, however, a major staging point for all biblical prophecy that follows. The central characters of the great drama are identified, and the plot begins to take shape. (1) Canaan will be subdued and turn to the God of Israel in faith (9:25–26). Henceforth, the Canaanite nations will play a central role in the prophetic picture of the last battle. (2) The people of the line of Shem (Israel) will be God's chosen people. They will serve the only true God, "the LORD, the God of Shem." Through them will come the blessing. This prepares us for God's election of Abraham that soon follows. (3) The people of the line of Japheth will "live in the tents of Shem." That means the sons of Japheth will conquer the sons of the line of Shem in war. Thus the "enmity" between the seed of the serpent and the seed of the woman is defined as a warfare between the line of Shem and the line of Japheth—between Israel and the nations. God is behind this warfare. He will "extend the territory of Japheth" (Gen. 9:27)! What is missing is a clear word about the ultimate victory of the people of God. That victory is the theme of numerous poetic passages in the rest of the Bible.

Paradise Regained: The Last Battle (Part 2)

A number of poetic texts in Scripture build on the theme of the last battle. In Genesis 49:8–12, for example, a mighty "Lion King" will arise from the tribe of Judah, defeat Israel's enemies, establish a universal kingdom, and restore God's creation to the prosperity it once enjoyed in the Garden of Eden.

In Numbers 24:7–9, that same king will arise victoriously over the kingdom of Gog. Our translations of verse 7 read, "Their king will be greater than Agag." But the earliest manuscripts of the Old Testament read, "Their king will be greater than Gog." At one time there must have been a dispute over the identity of the king's future enemy. If it is Agag, then the likely reference is to David, because his kingdom ruled over Agag (1 Sam. 15:8). If it is Gog, however, then the reference is more likely to the future king who will defeat the famed, but as yet unidentified, eschatological king, Gog (Ezek. 38:17). That messianic king will bring God's people out of the nations in a "new exodus," and, like a raging bull, he will defeat the enemy (Num. 24:8). He will bring to God's people the fulfillment of the promises to Abraham. Like the promised "offspring" of Genesis 3:15, he will crush the head of his enemies and rule over the nations.

A further reference to the last battle and the rise of the victorious king is found in Isaiah 34:1–15. There, in images drawn from the poetic texts of the Pentateuch, Isaiah describes the battle scenes of the Lord's final judgment on the nations. Isaiah then calls on his readers to examine for themselves the earlier prophecies of the last battle recorded in "the scroll of the LORD" (34:16). His promise is that not one prophetic word will go unfulfilled.

Perhaps the most notorious battle scene in all prophetic literature is Ezekiel 38–39, the battle between God and the nations who have united against Israel. As in Numbers 24:7, the archenemy of God is the infamous "Gog of the land of Magog" (Ezek. 38:2). The battle comes in a section dealing with the time of future blessing for Israel (chs. 33–48), falling between Ezekiel's account of the restoration of the house of David (chs. 33–35) and the restoration of the Jerusalem temple (chs. 40–48). The future Israel has returned from exile and their enemies have been destroyed (chs. 25–32). They are united again as one people, living in peace under the reign of a Davidic king (chs. 36–37) and enjoying fellowship with God in the newly rebuilt temple. Ezekiel 38–39 recounts an unexpected invasion of the Promised Land from the nations of the north, whose names are symbolic of the forces of the Antichrist, forces of evil and destruction. Attempts to identify some of these nations with modern countries are doubtful.

Paradise Regained: The Last Battle (Part 3)

The last battle is again described in Zechariah 14:1–21, where the Lord says, "I will gather all the nations to Jerusalem to fight against it" (14:2). To this the prophet adds, "Then the LORD will go out and fight against those nations, as he fights in the day of battle" (14:3). It will be a fierce battle (14:12–15), and the nations will be defeated. On that day a time of eternal peace will ensue: "The LORD will be king over the whole earth," (14:9) and "the survivors from all the nations that have attacked Jerusalem will go up year after year to worship the King, the LORD Almighty" (14:16).

Zechariah's contemporary, Daniel, also records a vision of the last battle, in which the eternal kingdom of God is to be established after the defeat of the Antichrist. In the last days a terrible "beast" will arise and oppress the nations and Jerusalem (Dan. 7:7). From that "beast with ten horns" will arise a "little horn," the Antichrist. In Daniel's interpretation, the beast and the little horn represent powerful, ungodly nations, who will attack the people of God (7:17, 19–21). Daniel's vision draws its basic images and themes from God's words to the serpent in Genesis 3:15, "I will put enmity between you and the woman, and between your offspring and hers," and that the seed of the woman will ultimately crush the head of the serpent. Thus Daniel sees that "the beast was slain and its body destroyed and thrown into the blazing fire" (Dan. 7:11). After that, the messianic Son of Man receives the kingdom from God, the Ancient of Days (7:13), and "his dominion is an everlasting dominion that will not pass away" (7:14). Thus "the saints of the Most High will receive the kingdom and will possess it forever" (7:18).

Daniel's vision makes a significant contribution to the theme of the last battle. It not only graphically portrays the defeat of the Antichrist, but it also highlights the central role of the messianic King who comes in the last battle to establish God's kingdom. Jesus and the New Testament authors make constant use of that imagery. It reaches its fullest expression in John's vision at the close of Revelation. There, in a vast assortment of biblical images, John describes the coming of Christ to defeat the enemy in the last battle (Rev. 19:11–21). Jesus is seen riding out of heaven on a white horse, accompanied by "the armies of heaven" (19:11, 14; cf. Dan. 7:13–14). Curiously, the sword that Christ wields comes "out of his mouth" (Rev. 19:15), just as in John's first vision of Christ (1:16). This suggests that the imagery of the last battle has, at least in part, been spiritualized to refer to the victorious power of God's word. Christ slays the enemy with that word (19:21).

Paradise Regained: The Slain Victor

An important part of the biblical picture of "Paradise Regained" is that the Redeemer who defeats the enemy and opens the way for returning to the good land is himself fatally wounded in the process. That aspect of the picture is evident already in Genesis 3:15b, where the Lord warns the serpent, "He will crush your head, and you will strike his heel." In crushing the head of the serpent, the promised offspring will suffer a fatal wound from the serpent. Although warfare is a constant theme, the notion of the death of the Redeemer does not, for the most part, play a central role in the Old Testament. At certain key places, however, it does come to the fore.

Isaiah's prophecy of the Suffering Servant is one of those cases. Throughout the second half of Isaiah, the prophet increasingly focuses our attention on the activities of the "servant of the LORD." At some points the "servant" is Israel, God's chosen people (e.g., Isa. 49:3), but it is a mistake to think that the servant is always Israel. Sometimes he is viewed as an individual, distinct from the people of God, who carries out God's work on behalf of Israel. In 49:5b, for example, the Servant of the Lord is called to "bring Jacob back to him and gather Israel to himself." Here the Servant cannot represent the people of God. A thematic parallelism seems to be intentionally established within this book between God's past and present work with Israel and God's future work with his Servant. It is not unusual within the prophetic texts to see God's purposes with Israel linked to his plans for the messianic King.

The central picture of the Servant of the Lord in Isaiah is found in the Suffering Servant of chapter 53. Here the Hebrew text is clear that the Servant is not Israel. The prophet, for example, says of him, "Just as there were many who were appalled at *you—his* appearance was so disfigured beyond that of any man" (52:14). Since the pronoun "you" refers to the people of Israel, the Servant cannot here be identified with the people. He is, rather, contrasted with the people. Some translators have changed the pronoun to "him" (cf. NIV note), thereby identifying the Servant with Israel, but the Hebrew does not support it. The sense of the verse is, "Just as you, O Israel, were disfigured, so also was my servant." The Servant is the slain victor.

The Servant of the Lord in Isaiah 53 was "pierced for our transgressions, he was crushed for our iniquities . . . and by his wounds we are healed" (53:5). He died as a "guilt offering," since "it was the LORD's will to crush him and cause him to suffer" (53:10). He "poured out his life unto death" (53:12). The death of the victorious warrior thus plays a central role in God's plan of redemption. He is "the Lamb that was slain from the creation of the world" (Rev. 13:8).

Paradise Regained: Resurrection and Restoration

Implicit in the idea of a slain Redeemer is the hope of resurrection, restoration, and eternal life. Scripture contains the recurring theme that at the end of the world God will raise up all the dead, and he will restore and transform their physical bodies. They will be given immortality and will stand in judgment before God.

In the Genesis account of the Fall, humanity forfeited eternal life (Gen. 3:24). Beyond God's promises, there was little hope left. Yet a basis for hope remained within that narrative, in that the "tree of life" was not destroyed. God merely placed angels in its path to keep it out of human hands. Though subtle, hope remained that God would reopen the path to the tree of life. That, in fact, is what the Bible is all about.

That same focus on eternal life reappears in the last chapters of the Bible. In the new heavens and new earth, "the tree of life" is again found in the midst of God's Paradise, the new Jerusalem. Its leaves "are for the healing of the nations" (Rev. 22:2). This is John's way of saying that humanity will then eat of the tree and live forever. The concept of restoration thus describes the relationship between the first chapters of the Bible and the last. What was lost has been regained. What was offered but rejected has now been accepted. Between these two "bookends," the Bible offers fallen humanity their only hope—the hope of a future resurrection.

The idea of a physical, earthly resurrection comes to full expression at several key points in the Bible. The book of Job, which concentrates on the abject misery of the human condition, gives one of the clearest expressions of that hope. Though he felt the heavy hand of God on him, Job did not give up hope beyond the grave. He said, "I know that my Redeemer lives, and that in the end he will stand upon the earth. And after my skin has been destroyed, yet in my flesh I will see God" (Job 19:25–26). Isaiah proclaimed to Israel that in the last day, "your dead will live; their bodies will rise. You who dwell in the dust, wake up and shout for joy" (Isa. 26:19). David also, contemplating the death of the Lord's messianic King, did not despair at the finality of death. His "heart [was] glad" and his "tongue rejoice[d]" (Ps. 16:9). Why? Because David had hope in the resurrection of the Lord's Anointed as well as his own (16:10–11). Likewise, Daniel received hope in the resurrection from the angel Michael, "Your people . . . will be delivered. Multitudes who sleep in the dust of the earth will awake: some to everlasting life, others to shame and everlasting contempt" (Dan. 12:1–2). In his own resurrection, Christ was the first of all humanity who were yet to be raised at the end of history. The Bible thus calls him the "firstfruits of those who have fallen asleep" (1 Cor. 15:20). Many more will follow.

Summary of Biblical Prophecy in the Pentateuch

The Pentateuch is not a series of books—Genesis, Exodus, Leviticus, Numbers, and Deuteronomy—but a single book with a single purpose. Its central subject matter is the exodus of Israel from Egypt and God's covenant with them at Mount Sinai. The author introduces this subject with creation and God's dealings in the early history of humanity (Gen. 1–11). He then recounts a series of stories about Israel's ancestors: Abraham, Isaac, Jacob, and Jacob's twelve sons (chs. 12–50). At the conclusion of the Pentateuch, the author recounts the final words of Moses to the new generation of Israelites, who are about to enter the Promised Land.

Does the overall sense of the Pentateuch fit into the prophetic scheme, and if so, how? The Pentateuch is in fact the foundation on which the entire prophetic view rests. As we have suggested earlier in this book, the prophetic view of the future is grounded in the Pentateuch's view of God, nature, and history. It represents God's design in creation as an act of grace. God created humanity for fellowship and worship. In God's providence, however, humanity rejected God's plan and sought to find blessing and meaning apart from God. But God was faithful to his original purposes and promised to restore humanity through the work of a Redeemer, laying out his plan in a series of covenants.

Central to the prophetic view of the Pentateuch are the covenants God made with Abraham and Moses. In the Abrahamic covenant, God promised to give the seed of Abraham the land of Canaan and to make them the source of blessing for all humanity. He planned to accomplish that purpose by raising up a king and a kingdom. That kingdom would be the Davidic kingdom, through which God intended to raise up a victorious Redeemer, who would defeat the forces of evil and bring peace and blessing to God's creation. Ultimately that King would defeat Satan, crushing the serpent's head (Gen. 3:15). The promise of a coming Redeemer is sustained throughout the Pentateuch in several strategically located poetic texts, which repeatedly turn the reader's attention to the ultimate victory promised in the arrival of the coming King.

A second central element in the prophetic message of the Pentateuch is the writer's portrayal of the failure of the Mosaic covenant. Though in itself a good covenant, the people proved unable or unwilling to fulfill its requirements. Something else was needed. Thus we are directed beyond the Mosaic covenant to a new covenant, only hinted at in the Pentateuch but fully explained in the later prophetic books. That new covenant was the promise of a new heart (Deut. 30:6) and an eternal redemption.

Summary of Biblical Prophecy in the Historical Books

One does not usually think of the Old Testament historical books (Joshua through Nehemiah) as a source of biblical prophecy. But these books were written for precisely that purpose. Though the writers were interested in their national history, their primary concern lay in the lessons that the history of Israel held for the future. They knew that God had made promises to his people and that the fulfillment of those promises remained an ever-present hope in their day. Much of the strength to endure hardships, such as the destruction of Jerusalem and the ensuing Babylonian captivity, was drawn from their trust in God's faithfulness.

The composition of the historical books grew largely out of the catastrophe of the destruction of Jerusalem and the Exile, explaining what that destruction meant to Israel's relationship with God. The author of Lamentations expressed the sense of dismay and shock that had overcome the nation: "Restore us to yourself, O LORD . . . renew our days as of old" (Lam. 5:21). Then, almost in complete resignation, he added, "unless you have utterly rejected us and are angry with us beyond measure" (5:22). That verse is so dismal in its hope for the future that later Hebrew scribes laid it down as a rule that verse 21 should be repeated after this verse so that the book would not end on such a note of despair.

The historical books addressed this state of mind. Did the destruction of Jerusalem and the loss of the Promised Land mean that God had utterly cast off his people? Was there a future? What had happened to all the promises God had made in the past? In their answer, the historical books insist that God had not forsaken Israel. There was a solid rock to which Israel could still attach their hope—the promise that God had made to the house of David (2 Sam. 7). Though the Davidic kings had proved faithless, God would not abandon his promise. A future remained for Israel because a future King would someday arise out of the house of David. That King was the Messiah, and the authors of the historical books set out to show that he had not yet come. No one in Israel's past—not even the greatest of their kings, King David himself—could be viewed as the Messiah. Thus, in reading the Old Testament historical books, one must be sensitive to the larger theme of each book—God's promise to David. Joshua is a picture of the coming messianic king. The judges picture the Messiah. The lives of David and Solomon foreshadow the life of one greater than they. Their kingdoms provide a glimpse of the reign of that king.

Summary of Biblical Prophecy in the Poetic Books

Many books in the Old Testament contain poetic sections. Poetry is frequently used in narrative books to highlight the messianic hope those books are trying to portray (e.g., 1 Sam. 2:10b), in the same way as in a musical, the songs help further the main themes of the drama.

The book of Psalms, on the other hand, is thoroughly poetic—that is to say, it is almost entirely musical. Many psalms express Israel's hope in the coming Messiah, but in a variety of ways. Individual psalms sing about Israel's king, priests, worshipers at the temple, and the everyday life of the pious Israelite; yet they do not always look as if they are concerned with the future messianic King. Often, however, these poetic psalms contain bits and pieces of additional narration. The music stops, so to speak, and we hear the voice of someone speaking. Such elements of narration highlight the messianic importance of a psalm.

Perhaps the analogy of an opera will help us understand the process. The psalms, like an opera, are mostly musical or poetic. Occasionally, however, as in an opera, the music stops and someone speaks, which serves to orient the reader to the central plot and the larger themes of the drama. The book of Psalms as a whole, then, has a plot structure and a central theme, which are focused on the prophetic hope of the coming Messiah. When the music stops and the speaking begins, we hear the theme of the Davidic covenant. The narrator, as it were, is reminding the reader of what the book of Psalms is all about—the coming Messiah.

Though an individual psalm may express a specific sentiment about Israel's earthly kings or the worship of God at the temple, within the context of the whole book each psalm plays a larger role by presenting a specific aspect or feature of the picture of Christ. Psalms is so well constructed that the average reader usually does not notice when the poetry of a psalm is broken by a piece of narration. But one can often spot these narrative breaks by looking for their content. Since their chief concern is to link the psalms to God's promises to David (i.e., the Davidic covenant), the writers frequently focus the reader's attention on that promise and on the importance of the city of Zion. In Psalm 133:3, for example, the poetic part is about the dew that flows down the slopes of Mount Hermon. But a small piece of narrative that speaks about Mount Zion has been inserted into the poetic line. The result is a well-formed psalm that is clearly speaking about God's promise of blessing to the house of David—the Messiah.

Summary of Biblical Prophecy in the Prophetic Books

Like the book of Psalms, the prophetic books are composed primarily of poetry, through which Israel's prophets delivered words of judgment and salvation. Those words were apparently written down by scribes, or disciples, who accompanied the prophets. They were then collected and recorded into books. The authors of these books were deeply interested in the messianic meaning of the prophets' words. Since their poetic words were often profound—one might even say, at times obscure—the authors occasionally went to some lengths to clarify and elucidate them for their readers.

Those explanations, as might be expected, usually centered around God's promise to the house of David and the messianic King. Sometimes the explanations consisted merely of the way in which the prophet arranged the message. They juxtaposed words of judgment, for example, with words of salvation and hope, showing that beyond Israel's experience of divine judgment lay the hope of redemption. The experience of divine wrath, such as the destruction of Jerusalem and exile to Babylon, did not mean an end to God's promises. God would remain faithful to his promises and would establish a kingdom through the Messiah. Hope in God's promise to David (2 Sam. 7) was thus transformed into an eager expectation of the coming of the Messiah.

Another way in which the words of the prophets elucidated their message is from the overall structure they gave their books. By and large, prophetic books follow a threefold pattern.

(1) Words of judgment against Israel and Judah form the first series of messages.

(2) Words of judgment against the nations form the middle section. These words are important to the prophetic message because they reflect God's commitment to the Abrahamic covenant, in which God promised that blessing and salvation would come to the nations through the "seed" of Abraham. Those who cursed Abraham, God would curse; those who blessed him, God would bless. The prophets thus proclaimed words of judgment against the nations because they neglected the salvation offered to them. God was not merely interested in the nation of Israel or the tribe of Judah. He was concerned about all the nations. He would judge them, just as he judged Israel. If, however, they turned to him, he would send them a Redeemer.

(3) The prophetic books close on a note of the reestablishment of the kingdom of David and the coming of the Messiah. The message is cast in the broadest terms possible, which included Israel, Judah, and all the nations.

Summary of Biblical Prophecy
in the Wisdom Books

The book of Proverbs has a discernible shape that reveals its messianic interest. The prologue (Prov. 1–9) is an extended apologetic for the value and importance of seeking wisdom. The body (chs. 10–24, plus an addition, chs. 25–29) is a selection of wise sayings, gathered for study and meditation. The conclusion of the book, which consists of several parts (30:1–33; 31:1–9; 31:10–31), tries to apply the wisdom embodied in the book in specific situations.

The wisdom portrayed in Proverbs is that of David's son, Solomon. The Davidic covenant thus forms the interpretive background. But there is another Son who emerges from this book. That Son is "one like Solomon," who is the personification of wisdom itself. We see him emerge within the literary strategy of the book. The author gives a close look at divine wisdom in chapter 8. "Wisdom" is a person who was with God at creation (8:22). This wisdom says, "When [God] marked out the foundations of the earth . . . I was the craftsman at his side" (8:29–30). By picturing wisdom as a person with God at creation, the author raises the question, "Who is this individual?" As the book closes, he returns to this person and supplies an answer—surprisingly in the prophetic oracle of Agur (30:1–6) rather than in a "wise saying."

Agur's wisdom comes to him as an oracle, that is, by direct revelation from God. For that reason the content of his "saying" goes beyond what has been given in the book so far. His words interpret several earlier passages of Scripture. When he asks, "Who has gone up to heaven and come down?" he is alluding to Moses' words in Deuteronomy 30:12, "Who will ascend into heaven. . . ?" (cf. Rom. 10:6). When he asks, "Who has gathered up the wind in the hollow of his hands? . . . Who has established all the ends of the earth?" he is alluding to the role of "wisdom" personified as a "craftsman" in Proverbs 8:27–30. In both passages Agur raises the question of the identity of the One who is with God and who brings wisdom from God.

In the following verses, Agur identifies this One as the "son" of God (30:4b) and "the word of God" (30:5). He gives us a picture of the Son of God, living with God as Wisdom personified and bringing God's word to us—a picture much like Daniel 7:14, where the Son of Man, who is with God in the heavenlies, brings God's kingdom to humanity in the last days. In this way, the author of Proverbs turns his reader's attention to Israel's future messianic hopes. The wisdom embodied in the sayings of Solomon becomes emblematic of the Wisdom of the divine Son of God known in the other biblical texts. The practical wisdom of the book of Proverbs thus aids in providing the way of escape in the coming Day of Judgment (30:5).

Prophecy in the New Testament

Summary of Biblical Prophecy in the Gospels

The four Gospels share a common perspective. They were written from the viewpoint that the crucified and risen Christ had ascended into heaven and was awaiting his return to earth. One of the central concerns in each Gospel is the return of Christ and the establishment of his kingdom. Each one makes the unique contribution to that theme.

Matthew's Gospel shows that Jesus was the promised Davidic King, sent from God, who offered his kingdom to the heirs of the Abrahamic covenant. A remnant of God's people received his kingdom, but it was rejected by the nation as a whole. The promise of the kingdom was thus delayed until Christ's return. When he does return, all the promises of God to Abraham and David will be fulfilled. The final discourse of Jesus (chs. 24–25) focuses on his return and the events that surround it. The book of Matthew is also about the church. The delay in establishing Christ's kingdom did not mean that God had forsaken those who did put their trust in him. Jesus established the church as the "mystery" form of his coming kingdom. It represented the promised kingdom in its spiritual reality only; the physical messianic kingdom, promised in the Old Testament, was yet to come.

The first words of Jesus that Mark records is the imminence of the kingdom of God (Mark 1:14–15). The only full-length teaching of Jesus in Mark is the discourse in Mark 13, which betrays Mark's interest in the "last days" and Jesus' role in fulfilling Israel's eschatological hope. The major turning point in Mark's portrayal of Jesus is Peter's confession, "You are the Christ'" (8:29). After this the focus of the Gospel is on the death and resurrection of Christ: "He then began to teach them that the Son of Man must suffer many things and be rejected . . . and that he must be killed and after three days rise again" (8:31).

Luke's Gospel shows that the Davidic King (Luke 1:31–33) comes to Jerusalem, but his kingdom is rejected (19:28–37, 41). Only his disciples recognize him as "the king who comes in the name of the Lord" (19:38). To the rest "it is hidden" (19:42). Jesus weeps, knowing what great blessings Israel could have had and what judgment lies ahead (19:41–45). There will be wars. Jerusalem will be destroyed by the Gentiles, and her people will be "taken as prisoners to all the nations . . . until the times of the Gentiles are fulfilled" (21:24). After this, the Son of Man will return, as foretold in the book of Daniel, "in a cloud with power and great glory" (21:27).

John's intention in writing his Gospel was to show that "Jesus is the Christ" (John 20:31), with the hope that people will believe in him. Particularly important is his identification of Jesus as the King of the Jews (18:36–37; 19:19–22). Jesus was recognized as the promised King, as the Messiah, and as the Son of Man who received the kingdom (Dan. 7:9–14).

Summary of Biblical Prophecy in the Book of Acts

As Acts begins, Luke shows that before Jesus' ascension, he spent forty days teaching his disciples about the kingdom of God (Acts 1:3). The disciples raised a central question: "Lord, are you at this time going to restore the kingdom to Israel?" (1:6). The book of Acts is intended as an answer to this question. At the end (28:31) Paul was preaching "the kingdom of God" in Rome and teaching about the Lord Jesus Christ. There is little question, then, that the establishment of the church and the spread of the gospel is linked to the beginning of the reign of the kingdom.

On the other hand, Paul was preaching about the kingdom of God *in Rome*, the capital of the Gentile world, not in Jerusalem. In fact, Acts clearly suggests that the center of the church, and hence the kingdom of God, had moved from Jerusalem to Rome. Thus Acts answers the disciples' question in 1:6 both positively and negatively. Negatively, the kingdom has not yet been restored to Israel. Positively, the kingdom has been established. As Jesus himself said to his disciples, "It is not for you to know the times or dates the Father has set by his own authority" (1:7). That coming kingdom is the one promised to David (2 Sam. 7)—a point Luke had already developed at Jesus' birth: "The Lord God will give him the throne of his father David, and he will reign over the house of Jacob forever; his kingdom will never end" (Luke 1:32–33).

Luke's treatment of Peter's speech in Acts 2 raises an important question. When Peter saw the signs around him of the coming of the Holy Spirit, he announced to those in Jerusalem, "This is what was spoken by the prophet Joel" (2:16). Peter then quoted a lengthy passage from Joel that spoke of the establishment of the messianic kingdom. Some understand Peter to be saying that the church, which was initiated at Pentecost, is the kingdom promised to David. Others point out that Peter stopped quoting Joel before he came to the part about the restoration of "the fortunes of Judah and Jerusalem" (Joel 3:1). Thus Peter did not mean that all Joel's prophecies were fulfilled at Pentecost—only the promise of the coming of the Holy Spirit.

The importance of this passage, however, does not rest simply with what Peter said at Pentecost. As important as that was, the real question is what Luke, the author of Acts, intended to say in the strategy of his book. The important point is that Peter made another speech in the next chapter (Acts 3:11–26), in which he clearly believed the messianic kingdom was still yet to come to Israel (3:19–21). Thus, though he believed the Joel prophecies were in some sense fulfilled at Pentecost, he still looked to the future for the coming of the Davidic kingdom.

Summary of Biblical Prophecy in the Letters

The New Testament letters were written within the context of the eager anticipation of the return of Christ. A central theme in Romans is: How does the gospel affect God's covenant promises to Israel? Do they still play a role in his plans? Paul's answer is that God intends to keep his covenant promises and that one day, Israel will turn to Christ in faith (Rom. 11:12–32). That they are experiencing a partial hardening, thus allowing for the inclusion of the Gentiles into God's plan, was previously unknown in the Scriptures. But at some future day Israel as a nation will be saved by believing in Jesus Christ as Savior. Scholars differ about the status of this believing nation of Israel in God's overall program. Some hold that when they believe, the Israelites will become a part of the church as the true Israel. Others hold that their belief will signal the fulfillment of the Old Testament promises to physical Israel, and they will belong to the Davidic kingdom over which Christ will rule (Isa. 2:2–4; 60:1ff.; 62:2; Zech. 9:22–23).

In 1 Thessalonians, Paul focuses on the eager expectation of his churches for the Lord's return. One matter that needed clarification was the timing of his return and the sequence of events, so Paul summarizes the events that will surround the return of Christ. Jesus, who himself died and rose again, will come down out of heaven, with a shout and the sound of a trumpet (1 Thess. 4:13–14). Then the "dead in Christ" will rise from their graves to meet him (4:15–16). After that, those Christians living at the time will rise into the air to meet him (4:17). When will this occur? No one knows; it will take most by surprise. But his true followers will be ready, for they will be watching and waiting (5:1–11).

The Thessalonian church experienced hardship and persecution, but they remained steadfast in their faith. In the midst of their troubles, rumors started circulating that Jesus had already returned. Paul thus wrote a second letter to comfort these faithful Christians and to affirm that though Jesus had not yet appeared, their hope in his soon return was not misplaced. He would return, establish his kingdom, and judge the world.

Central to Paul's understanding of Christ's return in 1 Corinthians is the concept of the resurrection (1 Cor. 15:23–28). Like Jesus in the Gospels, Paul's basic text is the Son of Man passages in Daniel 7 and 12. When Christ returns (1 Cor. 15:23b), those who belong to him will rise from the dead (15:23c), which will mark the coming of the end (15:24a). Christ will return to destroy "all dominion, authority and power" (15:24c), reign "until he has put all his enemies under his feet" (15:25)—including death itself (15:26)—and then "hands over the kingdom to God the Father" (15:24b). Paul's view of this future kingdom is the same as that of Jesus (Matt. 24).

Summary of Biblical Prophecy
in the Book of Revelation

The book of Revelation is about the final cataclysmic events that will yet transpire on the earth. Its central character is Jesus, "the faithful witness, the firstborn from the dead, and the ruler of the kings of the earth" (Rev. 1:5). These titles stress his death, resurrection, and exaltation over believers as well as his ultimate victory and exaltation over the nations.

In his first vision, John sees Jesus as "someone 'like a son of man'" (Rev. 1:13), who in Daniel's vision comes to judge the saints (Dan. 7:9–10). As in Daniel, divine judgment comes first, and then the Son of Man establishes his kingdom. It is likely that the churches addressed by Christ in Revelation 2–3 represent all churches at all times.

Revelation 4–19 contains a rich assortment of events, described in apocalyptic language. John sees the throne room of heaven and a scroll with seven seals, opened by the Lamb of God one seal at a time (chs. 4–7). Each seal brings with it a cataclysmic event. Then comes the blasts of seven trumpets (chs. 8–11), followed by a battle scene with great beasts and wicked powers (chs. 12–14), a vision of seven plagues (chs. 15–16), and the fall of Babylon (chs. 17–19). Because of the symbolic language, their meaning is not always self-evident.

The symbolism of the book owes its interpretation to other portions of Scripture, such as Daniel 7, Ezekiel 38–39, and Matthew 24. It seems clear that these chapters describe Daniel's seventieth week (Dan. 9:27), what Revelation calls "the great tribulation" (Rev. 7:14). A time is coming when the world will have to account for its deliberate and rebellious rejection of Christ.

The fall of Babylon at the end of the book is accompanied by a battle of the armies of heaven, led by the one mounted on a white horse whose name is "the Word of God" (Rev. 19:11–16). This is a picture of Christ (cf. 20:4), "KING OF KINGS AND LORD OF LORDS" (19:16). He defeats the Antichrist, the false prophet, and the kings (19:17–21). The dragon is bound in chains and cast into the Abyss for one thousand years (20:1–3). When those years end, Satan (the dragon) is released, gathers together all the nations (Gog and Magog), mounts an attack against Jerusalem, but is defeated by fire from heaven and is cast into a burning lake of fire.

The Final Judgment is depicted as a great court session in which all the dead are gathered and the deeds of each are read off from the books kept in the court (Rev. 20:11–15; cf. Dan. 7:10). John then sees a new Jerusalem, in which God again lives with humankind, just as he did in the Garden of Eden in the beginning (Gen. 2). His kingdom is an eternal kingdom (Rev. 22:4–5). Like the Garden of Eden, a river flows through the city and waters the tree of life (22:1–2). In this city the curse of Genesis 3 has been removed (22:3).

Central Themes in Bible Prophecy

Restoration

A basic rule in understanding biblical prophecy is: "The last days are like the first." When the writers of Scripture looked to the future, they saw a time of restoration—God's plans to bring the world back to "the way things were." God created the world a good and perfect place; it did not need improvement. When humanity rebelled against him and the need for redemption took center stage, God set out to bring his creation back into line with his original purpose. To be sure, through the whole of the process, something new was added. God manifested himself as gracious, merciful, and good, and he is thereby glorified.

God also made humanity's place in his world more secure. In the beginning, the human race was not eternally secure. Although the Bible represents the man and woman as "very good" (Gen. 1:31) and morally perfect, there was the possibility of change. Adam and Eve could, and did, choose to forsake God and go their own way. They lost God's gift of Paradise. In the eternity planned for humanity in the future, however, there will be no opportunity for change. An eternal redemption has been offered, for which the price has been paid. The redeemed have been created as new creatures, and there is no longer the possibility of another falling away from God. To this extent, then, the eternal future is more than a mere restoration of the past.

But, having said that, it is important to remember that the future towards which God's plan of redemption is heading is a return to his purposes in the past. Thus the prophets continually return to the themes of the early chapters of the Bible—Genesis 1–3. When, for example, the Pentateuch speaks of God's covenants with nature, all humanity, and the people of Israel, its depiction of God's gift of the "good land" lies at the center of all his gracious acts. The "land" God created, the Garden of Eden, the Promised Land—they are all the same. God wants his creation to enjoy his blessings in the land he has created for them.

The biblical writers' focus on the Promised Land does not exclude God's gift of the whole earth as humanity's "place." The Promised Land is merely the centerpiece of God's good gift. As the prophets unfold their vision of the future, the land remains the centerpiece. Thus, humanity's opposition to God's plan and God's blessing is, throughout the Bible, cast in the picture of the warring nations mounting their attack against Jerusalem. Behind every picture of warfare lies God's words to the first rebel, the serpent, "I will put enmity between you and the woman, and between your seed and hers" (Gen. 3:15). The biblical imagery of the future is cumulative. Later visions build on and link earlier ones. In the entire process, however, the prophets never lose sight of God's original purposes in the beginning.

Redemption

The human race has fallen from its original state (Gen. 3). When the man and the woman sinned and rebelled against God, they were cast off from his presence and were barred from access to the tree of life. This meant they began to experience both spiritual and physical death. They were immediately aware, in their nakedness, of the shame and guilt of their sin. Their attempt to cover their nakedness is a picture of all subsequent human attempts to cover over sin and its effects. In their one act of disobedience, "sin entered the world ... and death through sin" (Rom. 5:12; cf. 6:23); "the result of one trespass was condemnation for all men" (5:18). In the Fall, human beings not only lost their original righteousness, they gained a corrupt nature. They were dead in their sins, and only through Christ are those sins forgiven (Col. 2:13).

In the midst of God's judgment of the man and the woman immediately after the Fall, the human race was not left without hope. God promised that humanity could find their way back to him through a Redeemer, who would crush the head of the serpent (Gen. 3:15) and thus restore them to that relationship with God they enjoyed before the Fall. As the Bible unfolds all that this promise entailed, we gain an increasing understanding of God's great plan of redemption.

(1) The Redeemer of humanity must be of the offspring of the woman (Gen. 3:15); that is, he must be a human being.

(2) In addition, the promised offspring, the one who would crush the head of the serpent, would be fatally wounded. The serpent would "strike his heel" as he crushed the serpent's head (Gen. 3:15b). Someone had to die as the penalty of humanity's rebellious sin (2:17).

(3) Furthermore, for the death of the Redeemer to be effective, that is, of eternal value, he had to be God: "When Christ came as high priest ... he did not enter by means of the blood of goats and calves; but he entered the Most Holy Place once for all by his own blood, having obtained eternal redemption" (Heb. 9:11–12). Underlying this necessity is the biblical concept of sacrifice: Life must be exchanged for life. "Through the sacrifice of the body of Jesus Christ once for all" (Heb. 10:10), Jesus has become "the atoning sacrifice for our sins" (1 John 2:2).

(4) God provided the sacrifice (Gen. 22:8, 13–14). At first, the sacrifice was that of goats and bulls (Lev. 16:13–25). But they were insufficient for the sins of the people (Ps. 51:16). The promised King would offer himself as a sacrificial lamb (Isa. 53:7). He would be God's servant, "pierced for our transgressions, he was crushed for our iniquities; the punishment that brought us peace was upon him, and by his wounds we are healed" (Isa. 53:5).

Messianism

God's promised Redeemer, the Messiah, was to be the offspring of the woman (Gen. 3:15), of Abraham (12:1–3), of Judah (49:8–12), and of David (2 Sam. 7:12–16). He was to come from the nation of Israel, God's chosen people (Neh. 9:7). He would be a king (Num. 24:7, 17) and would rule not only his own people, but also all nations (Ps. 2:8). His kingdom would be universal, and through him all the nations would be blessed (72:17). He would receive the kingdom from God alone (Dan. 7:13–14) and would establish it by defeating God's enemies in one last great battle (Ezek. 38:7–23; Dan. 7:26). God would then restore the heavens and earth to their original state by creating them anew (Isa. 65:27). The Messiah as the Mighty God of Israel would "reign on David's throne and over his kingdom . . . forever" (9:7).

The Old Testament messianic promise is fulfilled in the life, death, resurrection, and glorious return of the Lord Jesus Christ. The New Testament writers show that Jesus is the King, born in a manger; the prophet, rejected by his own people; and the high priest, who offered his own body as a sacrifice for humanity's sin. Jesus was born into the family of David—legally through Joseph (Matt. 1:6–16) and physically through his mother Mary (Luke 3:23–31). Jesus, the Redeemer, was not only a man; he was also the Son of God. At his birth, the angel Gabriel announced to Mary that "the holy one to be born will be called the Son of God" (Luke 1:35). To him was given "the throne of his father David, and he will reign over the house of Jacob forever; his kingdom will never end" (1:32–33).

Israel, the people of God, rejected their King (see John 1:11). Hence, the kingdom was "taken away" from them and "given to a people who [would] produce its fruit" (Matt. 21:43). Though his own disciples did not understand him at the time, Jesus taught them that he had to suffer many things, be rejected, be killed, and after three days rise again (Mark 8:31). On the evening of the celebration of the Passover (John 18:28), at the time of day when the lamb was to be slain (Matt. 27:46), Jesus was crucified. Like the Passover lamb, "not one of his bones [were] broken" (John 19:31–36; cf. Ex. 12:46).

Christ was buried, but after three days he rose from the dead (Luke 24:6) and ascended into heaven (Acts 1:9), from where he will return to establish his kingdom (Acts 1:11) at the end of the age "with power and great glory" (Matt. 24:30). Thus Jesus will come again as a mighty warrior, defeating the forces of evil and, finally, crushing the head (Rev. 19:15) of "that ancient serpent called the devil or Satan, who leads the whole world astray" (12:9; 20:2; cf. Rom. 16:20).

Israel and the Church

A central question in any attempt to understand biblical prophecy is the relationship between Israel and the church. Some simply equate the two, while others carefully distinguish them. If Israel and the church are the same, then the prophecies made to Israel are fulfilled in the church. If they are not the same, then God's promises to Israel of land and blessing are still in effect for them. Strictly speaking, the Bible defines Israel as the physical descendants of Abraham, Isaac, and Jacob. As a nation, God gave them leaders and laws (Ex. 19–Lev. 26). He brought them into the land of Canaan, delivered the land into their hands, and protected them from their enemies. As long as they trusted God and obeyed his commandments, he was with them and they prospered (Josh. 1:8). When they disobeyed God and followed after idols, he punished them (Judg. 2:10–15) and ultimately cast them off into exile (Josh. 23:15–16; 2 Kings 25).

Even after the Exile, God was gracious to Israel. He brought them back to their land (Ezra 1:1–2:68) and renewed his ancient promises to bless them (Zech. 6:9–15). God even promised to do a new work with Israel that would far exceed his promises to their fathers—the establishment of a new covenant (Jer. 31:31–32). He promised to rebuild the ancient kingdom of David (Jer. 33:15–26; Amos 9:11–15) and to fulfill his covenant with Abraham (Mic. 7:18–20).

When Mary announced the news of Jesus' birth, she sang, God "has helped his servant Israel, remembering to be merciful to Abraham and his descendants forever" (Luke 1:54–55). Even after Israel rejected Jesus and turned their backs on the gospel, the apostle Paul, himself an Israelite (Phil. 3:4–6), saw an irrevocable future for Israel in God's overall plan of redemption (Rom. 11:26). He spoke of Israel as an olive branch, "broken off" so that the Gentiles might be "grafted in." The church is thus sharing "in the nourishing sap from the olive root" (11:17).

But what about the "all Israel," who will be saved after "the full number of the Gentiles has come in" (Rom. 11:25)? Will they become a part of the church? Or will they turn to Christ as Israelites, the reestablished people of God, apart from the church? One's view of biblical prophecy is largely determined by the answer to this question. Many believe that the nation of Israel was the church in the Old Testament, but because the Jews rejected Christ and the gospel, the church is now primarily Gentile. Thus, "all Israel" being saved after the fullness of the Gentiles has come into the church means that there will be a national repentance of Israel and a large influx of Jews into the church. Others believe that in Romans 11, Paul envisions a future reinstatement of the nation of Israel as God's people, over against the church. Though the primarily Gentile church is the present means of God's work in the world, in the future, after the church has been taken out of the world during the Tribulation, Israel will again be the people of God.

The Tribulation

The Tribulation is a time toward the close of history in which God's wrath will be poured out on the earth in a final, cataclysmic period of seven years. The Old Testament prophecies that relate to the second coming of Christ contain numerous references to a time of affliction for God's people and the nations. Just as before their deliverance from Egypt and Babylon, Israel suffered affliction, so also Israel will again be afflicted by God's enemies. After their deliverance, the nations will be punished. Daniel, for example, in his vision of the four beasts and the Son of Man, mentions that the "little horn" (the Antichrist) will wage "war against the saints" and defeat them (Dan. 7:21). This will happen when the fourth beast subdues the whole earth and oppresses the "saints" of the Most High (7:25a). Daniel is then told that "the saints will be handed over to [the beast] for a time, times and half a time" (7:25b). After that period of time, their oppressors will be destroyed, and Israel will inherit an eternal kingdom (7:27).

Later, a further explanation is given to Daniel. God has decreed an extended period of time (483 years) for his people Israel and the city of Jerusalem (Dan. 9:24). At the end of that period, the Messiah will come, but he "will be cut off" and Jerusalem will be destroyed (9:25–26). A final period of seven years will commence with the rise of a ruler (the Antichrist), who will first enter into a covenant with Israel, and then will suddenly break off the covenant and commit a horrendous act of desecration in Israel's temple (9:27).

Paul speaks of this same ruler as the "man of lawlessness," who "sets himself up in God's temple, proclaiming himself to be God" (2 Thess. 2:3–4). He will work counterfeit miracles, signs, and wonders (2:9). John devotes considerable attention to the activities of the Antichrist. He is the "beast" who, with the "false prophet," carries out the work of Satan (Rev. 13). John describes their reign of terror as a time in which anyone not submitting to the authority of the beast will suffer persecution and death (13:16–17).

Some believe that during the Tribulation, God's people will continue to be the church, those who have put their faith in Christ. Christ will not return for them until the end of the seven-year Tribulation period. The church will then be "raptured" to meet Christ on his victorious return to establish his kingdom. Others believe the church will be removed from the world before the Tribulation. When Christ comes, the dead in him will arise, and together with those still living at the time, will be taken into the air to meet him (1 Thess. 4:13–18). After that time, after the church is taken off the earth, a time of great trouble will inflict those who remain on the earth.

The Rapture

In explaining the events that will accompany the Lord's return, Paul gives the following sequence: (1) The Lord will come down from heaven with a great shout and the blast of a trumpet (1 Thess. 4:16). (2) A great resurrection of the "dead in Christ" will immediately follow; they will rise up to meet Christ in the air (4:16b). (3) Those Christians still alive at that time will then "be caught up together with them in the clouds to meet the Lord in the air" (4:17). This event is called "the Rapture" (because early Bible translators used the Latin verb for "to be caught up," *rapto*).

The common view of the Rapture before the last century was that Paul is speaking in general terms about the return of Christ and about Christians' meeting him. He is not giving an exact description of a specific series of events but is addressing the question whether Christians who have died are at some disadvantage. Paul's answer is that they are not. Deceased Christians at the time of Christ's return will first be resurrected, and then those alive will be changed and go to be with Christ. Following Augustine, some have even maintained that all those raptured will first die, then be resurrected and receive an immortal body (cf. 1 Cor. 15:42–44). The Rapture is thus an instantaneous death, resurrection, and transformation of the living Christian.

Over the last hundred years, many Christians have tended to read their Bibles differently on this issue. Biblical prophecies are taken as face-value descriptions of real events. Thus, Paul's suggestion that Christians living at the time of Christ's return will be "caught up together ... in the clouds" (1 Thess. 4:17) has been understood in a physical and realistic way. If one conceives of Christ's return in the clouds as a real event, why not also understand the rapture of Christians in the same way? Many thus think Paul is speaking about a specific physical event that will accompany the return of Christ. All Christians, living and dead, will be caught up to meet Christ as he returns to establish his earthly kingdom.

Bible students have then set out to determine the precise sequence of the Rapture within the larger scheme of the events of Christ's return. The issue has centered on whether the Rapture precedes or follows the Tribulation. Those who believe the church will not go through the Tribulation see the Rapture as God's means for taking the church out of the world. The church will remain with Christ, in heaven, during the seven years of the Tribulation, and they return with him at the end. Those who believe the church will go through the Tribulation see the Rapture as God's means for rescuing the church at the close of the Tribulation.

The Millennium

The central theme of biblical prophecy is the kingdom of God. The prophets often returned to God's promises to establish his kingdom through the seed of Abraham and the house of David. In the Davidic covenant, God promised to make David's kingdom an eternal kingdom and to give his house (i.e., his dynasty) an eternal ruler (2 Sam. 7:16), who was to be one of his sons (7:12). The sign of his coming would be the building of the temple in Jerusalem (7:13).

When and how was David's eternal kingdom to be established? Obviously, David's eternal kingdom was not established in ancient Israel, for it ended in the Babylonian Captivity. Nor was David's kingdom rebuilt after the return from Exile. The angelic pronouncements at the birth of Christ make it clear that Jesus was and is the promised Davidic King, who came to establish the promised kingdom (Luke 1:32–33). Jesus' own preaching reinforced that idea, for he offered his kingdom to the heirs of the Abrahamic covenant (cf. Matt. 15:24). In the Gospels Jesus' kingdom was received by a remnant of God's people, but it was rejected by the nation as a whole. Then, in the book of Acts, we read that subsequent to his death, resurrection, and ascension, Jesus established the church. Is, then, the church the kingdom of God?

Insofar as God's kingdom is represented by God's presence and activity in the world, the church is the kingdom. If, however, one understands the kingdom of God as the messianic kingdom promised to David in 2 Samuel 7, then the church is not the kingdom—or, at least, not yet. Many theologians believe that the kingdom promised to David is still to be established physically here on earth. That kingdom was postponed when the Jews rejected Jesus as their Messiah, but it will be established when Christ returns.

The biblical picture of Christ's return is built on the imagery of Daniel 7:13–14. There the messianic King comes in the clouds in the sky to establish his kingdom, which extends over all the earth. In the final days of history, Christ will return to defeat Satan and establish an earthly kingdom for a thousand years (Rev. 20:4–6). That kingdom is called the Millennium (the Latin word *millennium* means "one thousand years"). After that millennial reign, all humanity will be judged and then enter into the eternal state. The righteous will dwell with Christ forever, and the wicked will go to eternal destruction. This view is called "premillennialism."

Many other theologians, however, view the church as the spiritual equivalent to David's promised messianic kingdom. When the Old Testament speaks of Christ reigning over an earthy kingdom, they understand that to mean Christ's spiritual rule today in the church. In other words, we are now in the Millennium. That position is known as "amillennialism."

Heaven

The word "heaven" means at least three things in the Bible. It refers to (1) the sky (Gen. 1:20); (2) the universe (1:14); and (3) the place where God (Isa. 66:1) and his angels (6:1–2) live. It is in this last sense that we are interested in the concept of heaven in Scripture.

Where is heaven? To the biblical writers, heaven is a place, and it is "up." For example, God always comes "down" from heaven (Ex. 19:18–20) and goes back "up" to heaven. Both Elijah (2 Kings 2:11) and Jesus (Acts 1:9–11) were taken "up" into heaven. Heaven is a part of this world of time and space. God hears our prayers "from heaven" (1 Kings 8:30b), and God is "in" heaven, even though heaven cannot contain him (8:27).

What is heaven? Primarily, it is a temple or palace from where God reigns over his world. The Old Testament tabernacle and temple were patterned after this abode (Ex. 25:9; 26:30; Heb. 8:1–2, 4–5).

Where do we go when we die? In general terms, the Old Testament speaks of dying as being "gathered to [one's] people" (Gen. 25:8); this place is called "Sheol." In the New Testament, those who die go either to "[Abraham's] side" or to "Hades" (see Jesus' parable about the rich man and Lazarus in Luke 16:19–31). These two places are separated by a "great chasm" (16:26). Elsewhere Jesus says, "In my Father's house are many rooms" (John 14:2). He is speaking here of the heavenly temple and is drawing on the vision of the prophet Ezekiel, who spoke of the new temple as having rooms for the priest's dwelling (Ezek. 40:38–47).

Where is Christ now? At the present time, he is in heaven, seated at the right hand of the Father (Mark 16:19; Luke 29:51; Acts 1:11; 2:32–36; Eph. 1:20; Heb. 8:1–2). This place is also called "paradise" (Luke 23:43). He will be there "until the time comes for God to restore everything" (Acts 3:21), that is, until Christ returns to establish his kingdom on earth.

What will heaven be like when Christ returns? God will renew the "heavens and earth" (Isa. 65:17; Rom. 8:21; 2 Peter 3:10–14). The heavenly city, "the new Jerusalem" (Rev. 21:2), the place prepared for us (John 14:2; 2 Cor. 5:1), will descend from heaven. Thus, "heaven," the place where we will live with Christ, will be on the "new earth"—just as the Garden of Eden was the place for God's fellowship with humanity in the beginning. The dead in Christ will be resurrected (1 Thess. 4:16), and those who are alive at the time will be transformed (1 Cor. 15:50–54; 1 Thess. 4:17). Christians have bodies, called "buildings," prepared for them that will last forever (2 Cor. 5:1); at Christ's return, we will put on those "spiritual bodies."

Theological Systems and Bible Prophecy

Covenant Theology

The theological systems that have most often influenced the study of biblical prophecy are covenant theology and dispensationalism.

Covenant theology is built around the idea of a "covenant," a legal agreement between God and the world. According to covenant theologians, God has established two basic covenants with the human race, the covenant of works and the covenant of grace, and he continues to work with human beings in the light of these two covenants.

In the covenant of works, God promised to bless humanity if they proved obedient to him. He established this covenant with the first man and woman in the Garden of Eden. They were commanded not to eat of the Tree of the Knowledge of Good and Evil. Had they met this condition of obedience, God would have graciously given them eternal life. But the covenant of works must not be seen as a "works salvation." It is merely a covenant that was to be put into effect by human obedience. But Adam and Eve disobeyed God and thereby broke the covenant of works. They thus faced the threat of eternal death.

While they were still in the Garden, God initiated the covenant of grace, in which he promised to provide redemption for the human race. That redemption was freely given to all who accepted it. To accept God's provision of salvation one had simply to believe in the gospel—to believe God's promise to provide a Redeemer. This promise was revealed to Adam and Eve even while they were hearing of their judgment from the covenant of works (Gen. 3:15). The content of the gospel has remained the same throughout history, though in earlier days it was not as directly and clearly stated as it is in the church today.

In covenant theology, the basic message of the gospel was administered in a variety of ways in Old Testament times. During the patriarchal period, the head of the family served as a priest, who offered the appropriate sacrificial offering for his household. In that offering Christ was typified and hence was the object of their faith. Circumcision was the sign of belonging to the covenant. After the Exodus, Moses received laws as a further means of implementing the covenant of grace. When Israel failed to keep the covenant, their prophets began to announce the arrival of a new covenant, in which the law of God would be written on the human heart and all nations would enjoy the promises once made to Israel. Jesus Christ came to establish the new covenant and to fulfill Israel's promises in the church. Since the church is now the people of God, all the promises to Israel (now understood spiritually) are now fulfilled in the church.

Dispensationalism

Dispensationalism shares many features with covenant theology, but there are also significant differences. Like covenant theologians, dispensationalists believe that God put Adam to a test in the Garden of Eden and that Adam failed the test by disobeying God. Hence, the promised gift of eternal life was lost to all his descendants. But rather than seeing God as immediately entering into a covenant of grace with Adam and Eve, dispensationalists see God as putting humanity to a whole series of new tests. Human history is thus marked by specific time periods, during which a particular kind of test is administered (dispensed) to all humanity and specifically to Israel, God's chosen people. These "tests" ("dispensations") are not like the "covenants" of covenant theology; they were not given as the basis of blessing and reward. Instead, they were given only to show that humanity is in constant need of God's grace.

Each test is distinct and administered to a specific group of people. God's covenant with Israel at Mount Sinai was thus a separate and distinct "dispensation" over against the "new covenant," which he promised to Israel in the future (Jer. 31:31–32). In the Sinai covenant, Israel was to obey the law written on tablets of stone; in the new covenant, Israel was to obey the law written on their hearts (Jer. 31:33–34; Ezek. 36:26–27). Such obedience was not the grounds for divine salvation and eternal life, but the means by which one's faith in God's free grace was demonstrated.

The distinction between the views of dispensationalism and covenant theology has led to a major difference in the way these two theological systems view Bible prophecy. Dispensationalists hold that the new covenant is promised to Israel in the future, not to the church as such. It was intended for Israel as a replacement of the Sinai covenant. Thus, all those promises that relate to the new covenant must still be fulfilled. The church may, and in fact, does, enjoy some of the blessings of the new covenant in the present dispensation (Heb. 8–10), but these are not fulfillments of Old Testament promises. The Old Testament prophecies of the coming kingdom of God began to be fulfilled in Christ's day, but after his death and resurrection, those fulfillments were "put on hold," until the days when Christ's return draws near. That is, when Israel rejected Jesus as their Messiah, God cast them off for a time—the "church age"—but he will not cast them off forever. When Christ returns to establish his kingdom here on earth, God will again work through his people Israel, and all the Old Testament prophecies will be fulfilled in the Millennium.

Glossary

Abrahamic Covenant

Genesis 12:1–3; 15:9–21; 17:1–14

God promised Abraham that his descendants would become a great nation and enjoy his blessing; through them the rest of humanity would be blessed. This Abrahamic covenant is the basis of God's dealings with Israel and all of humanity in the rest of the Bible. All God's present and future promises are fulfillments of God's promise to Abraham. Through the descendants of Abraham the Messiah came. The biblical basis of modern missions and evangelism is God's promise to bless "all the peoples on earth" (Gen. 12:3) through the descendants of Abraham, that is, through the Messiah, Jesus Christ. *See also* Blessing, Covenant

Atoning Sacrifice

See Sacrifices and Offerings (Atonement)

Babylonian Captivity

See Exile

Blessing

The concept of blessing is the Bible's way of expressing God's purpose and design for the creation of humanity. When God created the man and the woman, he blessed them, saying, "Be fruitful and increase in number; fill the earth and subdue it" (Gen. 1:28). This clearly entails the enjoyment of a full and enriched life of fellowship with God and one's own family. The Bible says elsewhere that children are a great reward from God: "Blessed is the man whose quiver is full of them" (Ps. 127:5). A key element in the biblical concept of blessing, according to the early chapters of Genesis, is the gift of eternal life. This was offered to all humanity in the Tree of Life (Gen. 2), but when the man and the woman forsook God's blessing and sought one of their own, they lost access to it (Gen. 3). The rest of the Bible is a story of God's gracious offer of the blessing of eternal life. The preeminent blessing that the Messiah brings to all humanity is "life forevermore" (Ps. 133:3) or "eternal life" (John 3:16).

Covenant

Strictly speaking, a covenant is a legal contract in which one or more parties bind themselves to certain agreements. Promises are made and faithfulness to the covenant is measured by the fulfillment of those promises. God made various covenants with humankind and his world. In Genesis, for example, God made a covenant with Noah and all living creatures that he would never again destroy the world with a flood (Gen. 9:8–11). This is called the Noahic Covenant. *See also* Abrahamic Covenant, Mosaic Covenant, Davidic Covenant, and New Covenant

Davidic Covenant

2 Samuel 7

When God chose David as king over Israel, he entered a covenant with him regarding the future of both his dynasty and kingdom. God promised that a son would be born to his house who would build a temple in Jerusalem and rule gloriously over the people of God. Initially, the fulfillment of that covenant appeared to lie in the reign of Solomon, the son of David, who built the first temple in Jerusalem. Solomon, however, proved unworthy of that honor, and the promised was passed on to the subsequent generations of Davidic kings, none of whom proved worthy of the promise. The hope for the fulfillment of the Davidic covenant was thus transferred to the future; or, to say it another way, from the beginning of the Old Testament Scriptures, the focus of God's promise to David was always on the future "seed" or descendant of David, who was the Messiah. Thus the Davidic covenant lies at the heart of the messianic prophecies of the Old Testament; those prophecies are fulfilled in the life and death of Jesus, the Son of David.

Eschatology

Throughout the Bible is a persistent hope that in the future God will intervene in the affairs of this world and do a mighty work by restoring creation and accomplishing redemption. This study is called *eschatology* (taken from the Greek word for the "last things," *eschaton*). God created all things good. But humanity rebelled; hence all of God's good creation was subjected to the curse. God's act of redemption in sending his Son to die on the cross removed the penalty of sin and provided for a new humanity and a new creation. The completion of those two new things lies in the future, when God will break into the present order of creation and renew all things. He began that work with the coming of Christ, but will finish it only when Christ returns to establish his kingdom. Thus, *eschatology* can refer to the first coming of Christ or to his second coming to establish his kingdom. The Old Testament does not divide the Messiah's coming into a first coming and a second coming; that became necessary only after the Messiah was rejected and the consummation of his kingdom was delayed. Thus an eschatological text in the Old Testament may find its fulfillment in the first coming or second coming of Christ. *See* Messianic

The Exile (or Babylonian Captivity)

The exile was a historical event in the life of the people of Israel, in which their country and cities were destroyed and they were taken captive into Babylon (this happened in the sixth century B.C.). This was more than a mere historical event, however, for it also meant that God, who had endured centuries of rebellion on the part of his chosen people, was finally bringing about the due penalty for Israel's sin. God is a just God—a God of mercy and a God of wrath. His mercy was shown in his long delay of sending Israel into captivity; his justice in the destruction of the nation by the Babylonians. The exile was of central importance to the biblical writers, for the Lord himself had become Israel's enemy. The nation, who had for many centuries assumed that God would never destroy his own people, now faced the horrible reality that they were living in a foreign land and were captive to a foreign people. Moreover, their own land lay in ruins. *See also* The Return from Captivity

Kingdom (Kingdom of God)

God is the King of all creation, and all creation is subject to him and his will. He cares for his world as a king cares for his subjects and realm. His law, the expression of his will, reigns throughout his realm. In the books of the Old Testament, God's kingdom is represented in his rule over the people of Israel. Israel was a theocracy (meaning "rule by God"; cf. Judg. 8:23). In the establishment of the Davidic kingship (*see* Davidic Covenant), the kingdom of Israel became the physical representation of the kingdom of God on earth, and God ruled through the house of David. The promised Son of David, the Messiah, was to rule over all the world from the throne of David (Ps. 2:8). In the Gospels, Jesus preached that the kingdom of God was on the verge of being established. Though he was rejected by his own countrymen and crucified by Rome, the New Testament writers do not give up hope that his kingdom will endure. The central message of the gospel is that those who put their faith in Christ become members of his kingdom and that the whole of his kingdom will be established at his future return.

Messiah, Messianic

Throughout the Bible is a recurring theme of fall and redemption (*see* Eschatology). God created the world good. But his world and its creatures rebelled and now stand in opposition to him. In God's grace, he promised to send a Redeemer—an individual who would defeat the forces of evil and establish a righteous kingdom (*see* Kingdom). This Redeemer, who would rule God's creation and all humanity, is variously described in the Bible. In the Old Testament he is identified as a king from the tribe of Judah or the house of David. He is a prophet like Moses, a priest like Melchizedek, or the "Son of Man" who will return in the clouds of the heavens to establish his universal kingdom. In the New Testament the Redeemer is Jesus.

In the Old Testament the title *Messiah* is rarely, if ever, used of this coming Redeemer—the reason being that the word *messiah* (meaning "the anointed one") is used in a number of different ways. For example, it was a common title for the political king. In the New Testament, Jesus is primarily known as the Messiah, though in its Greek form, *Christos* ("the Christ"). Because of this lack of uniform terminology in the Bible, it is best to use the term *messianic* rather than *Messiah*. The term *messianic* is used to describe any and all biblical passages that speak of a future redemption in light of an individual Redeemer.

Mosaic Covenant

Exodus 19–24

On several occasions throughout Israel's early history, God established, and renewed, a covenant between himself and his people. The central passages recounting that covenant are Exodus 19 and 24. In that covenant God promised Israel that they would be a great and wise nation if they would obey him and keep his commandments. Though Israel often transgressed the Mosaic covenant, as in the case of the Golden Calf (Ex. 32), God forgave them and continued his covenant relationship with them. Eventually Israel's rebellion caught up with them, however. The Mosaic covenant had stipulated (Deut. 4:26–27; 28:15–68) that if Israel failed to obey God's law, they would be carried away in exile from the Promised Land. That happened in the Babylonian captivity (*see* The Exile).

New Covenant

Jeremiah 31:31–34

As Israel's relationship with God under the Mosaic covenant progressed from bad to worse, God raised up prophets to proclaim that divine judgment for Israel lay just ahead if the people did not repent. Their failure to heed the prophets only served to seal the threat of judgment. God delivered his people over to their enemies, and they were taken into captivity (*see* Mosaic Covenant). But these same prophets who brought God's message of doom and destruction were also the heralds of another, more hopeful message—that this was not the end of their relationship with God, for God promised a new covenant. This covenant would not be like the Mosaic covenant, which presented Israel with a written law, with detailed stipulations that had to be kept. In the new covenant God's people would be changed. God would send his Spirit (Ezek. 36:24–28) and renew their hearts and minds (John 3:5–8). They would all obey God's will because it would be written on their hearts.

Central to the concept of the new covenant was the necessity of humanity's sin and guilt being atoned for once and for all. There was the need for a perfect redemption. This was accomplished by the death of Christ on the cross. Hence, on the eve of his death Jesus spoke of his crucifixion and his blood as the means of establishing the new covenant (Luke 22:20). *See* Sacrifices and Offerings (Atonement), Covenant

Noahic Covenant

See Covenant

Remnant

A remnant is a small select group, distinguished from a larger group by their faithfulness and sincerity. That concept is already present in the Flood narratives of Genesis, for Noah and his family formed a faithful remnant amid a generation that had turned its back on God. When God later chose Abraham, he intended to form a nation, which would be a remnant of sorts among all the families of the earth. This nation was to be a kingdom of priests and a holy nation (Ex. 19:6). But it soon became evident that not all of the descendants of Abraham would prove faithful and follow God's call to live a holy life. Thus early in the biblical texts the concept of a faithful remnant within the larger group of God's people developed. As the people of God drifted further from his way, the focus of God's promises began to shift onto the shoulders of this faithful remnant. In the later prophetic books of the Old Testament, the hope for the future focused almost entirely on the remnant. Through the concept of the remnant, the promises to the fathers could find fulfillment even though the nation as a whole might suffer divine wrath.

The Return from Captivity

The Babylonian captivity was a central event in the life of God's people (*see* The Exile). It meant that God's people were themselves experiencing God's wrath. But the biblical writers also stressed that God's wrath against his own people would not last forever. God, who had allowed his people to be taken to Babylon, would also bring them out of captivity and back into the Promised Land. This return was a central focus of the hope that the prophets put before the people. The prophet Jeremiah, for example, foresaw that the Babylonian exile would last only seventy years, after which God's people would return to the land; this happened when King Cyrus of Persia issued an edict that allowed all who desired to return to the Promised Land. Though there was great hope that the return from Babylon might mean the fulfillment of the messianic hopes of the people, that did not happen. The coming of the Messiah was projected into a much more distant future (see Dan. 9:24–27).

Sacrifices and Offerings (Atonement)

Central to the rituals and holy actions described in the Bible is the concept of atonement. A holy and righteous God cannot overlook wickedness or lawlessness. Numerous examples in the Bible demonstrate that the only just penalty for blatant disobedience to God's will is death (e.g., Gen. 2:17).

Human beings have strayed from God's way and sought their own means of finding blessing (*see* Blessing). But God is a gracious God (Ex. 34:6). In spite of Israel's repeated failures, he provided a means of substitution whereby the death rightly due sinful human beings was transferred to an innocent animal. The blood shed by that animal was accepted by God as a substitute for the blood of the guilty sinner. That system of sacrifice was God's gracious gift to atone for sin. The word *atonement* means, literally, "to be *at one* [atone] with."

There was, however, a latent inequity in its system of sacrifices. Already in the Old Testament that inequity is felt. David, for example, says in Psalm 51:15–16: "O Lord . . . you do not delight in sacrifice, or I would bring it; you do not take pleasure in burnt offerings." This same theme is picked up in the New Testament: "It is impossible for the blood of bulls and goats to take away sins" (Heb. 10:4). These sacrifices thus served more as a reminder of sin and the need for atonement than as the actual removal of guilt. They had to be repeated regularly in order to cover the guilt of the people. In other words, something more was necessary. That something, as the New Testament teaches, is "the sacrifice of the body of Jesus Christ once for all" (Heb. 10:10).

Sinai Covenant

See Mosaic Covenant

Tabernacle

The term *tabernacle* means simply "tent." The tabernacle was the tent in which God lived among his people. God is a holy God. Were he to live freely among his people, they would face the serious consequences of having a holy and righteous God in their midst. To safeguard the people and yet to ensure his own presence with them, God gave instructions to his people in the desert to build a dwelling for him. The primary purpose of the tabernacle was thus to provide adequate separation between God and the people. It was not to keep God from them, but keep them from improperly entering into his presence. The only proper entry of a sinful people into the presence of a holy God was through the blood of the sacrifice (*see* Sacrifices and Offerings [Atonement]). The construction of the tabernacle served as a basis for such sacrifices.

An important feature of the tabernacle was its portability. It was constructed so that it could be dismantled and carried along with the people. In that way God continued to live with Israel everywhere they were in the desert. They did not have to return regularly to Mount Sinai to meet with him. After they settled in the Promised Land, Israel built the temple, whose purpose was also to serve as a dwelling place for God. There he could be with his people, and they could come before him with sacrifices and offerings (cf. 1 Kings 8).

In the New Testament, the incarnation of Jesus is understood along lines similar to the tabernacle (John 1:14). When God became a human being, it was the ultimate act of condescension. God was no longer approached through the rituals of the tabernacle or temple; he was now living among us in bodily form.

The Torah (Pentateuch)

The Torah, the first section of the Old Testament, is made up of five parts. These parts—Genesis, Exodus, Leviticus, Numbers, and Deuteronomy—are usually considered individual books in their own right. In reality, they are merely five segments of the larger work called the *Pentateuch* (a Greek word meaning "five-part book"). The Hebrew word *Torah* means "instruction." The Torah is the foundational document of both the Old and the New Testaments. In it the central themes of the Bible are laid down and given their initial development. The subsequent books of the Bible develop these themes in a variety of ways.

Improve your Bible study skills with these Zondervan best sellers!

How to Read the Bible for All Its Worth
Second Edition
Gordon D. Fee and Douglas Stuart

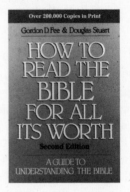

Discover the tools and techniques for getting
maximum return on your Bible study investment.
Respected professors Gordon D. Fee and Douglas
Stuart introduce insights from biblical scholarship
that help you confidently determine what Scripture said to its original listeners and what it says
to us today. Learn the difference between the
Psalms and the parables, Genesis and Revelation,
the prophets and the epistles; and find out what questions you need to ask
of each to accurately understand and correctly apply them. Over 300,000
copies in print!

Softcover: 0-310-38491-5

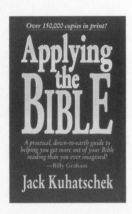

Applying the Bible
Jack Kuhatschek

Don't just study the Bible—apply it! Jack
Kuhatschek uses numerous illustrations and
examples to demonstrate a clear and reliable
method of applying the Bible, showing you
how to uncover the timeless principles of
Scripture—even in those passages that seem
meaningless today—and how to relate those
principles to your everyday life. Over 150,000
copies in print!

Softcover: 0-310-20838-6

**Look for Applying the Bible *and* How to Read the Bible for All Its
Worth *at your local Christian bookstore.***

ZondervanPublishingHouse
Grand Rapids, Michigan

A Division of HarperCollinsPublishers

http://www.zondervan.com

Here's your next step after the Zondervan Quick-Reference Library

The NIV Bible Companion
Alister E. McGrath

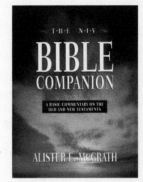

Learn the basics of the Bible with this easy-to-read commentary based on the most popular and understandable Bible translation: the New International Version (NIV).

Alister E. McGrath, one of today's leading evangelical scholars, begins with an overview of Scripture, showing you where to start reading and how to locate books, chapters, and verses. He then covers the entire Bible from Genesis to Revelation and demonstrates God's faithfulness throughout the turbulent history of Israel, the life, death, resurrection, and ascension of Jesus Christ, and the activity of the early church as it struggled to live out the faith in everyday life.

If you are a new believer or are considering becoming a Christian, you will appreciate Dr. McGrath's simple yet informed approach that assumes no previous Bible knowledge. If you are a more experienced believer, you will value how he places difficult Bible passages in their historical context and then shows how they can apply today.

Hardcover: 0-310-20547-6

Find The NIV Bible Companion at your local Christian bookstore.

ZondervanPublishingHouse
Grand Rapids, Michigan

A Division of HarperCollins*Publishers*

http://www.zondervan.com

More books by John Sailhamer

The NIV Compact Series

This four-volume series sits handsomely on your desk or bookshelf, ready to answer your Bible study questions quickly and authoritatively. If you read the NIV Bible, then you need this series.

NIV Compact Concordance, by John R. Kohlenberger III and Edward W. Goodrick

> 0-310-59480-4

NIV Compact Bible Commentary, by John Sailhamer

> 0-310-51460-6

NIV Compact Nave's Topical Bible, by John R. Kohlenberger III

0-310-40210-7

NIV Compact Dictionary of the Bible, by J. D. Douglas and Merrill C. Tenney

0-310-33180-3

The Pentateuch as Narrative
A Biblical-Theological Commentary

Understand the first five books of the Bible as their author originally intended. Dr. Sailhamer presents the Pentateuch as a coherent whole, revealing historical and literary themes that appear clearly only when it is read this way. A fresh look at the beginnings of the nation of Israel and the earliest foundations of the Christian faith.

Softcover: 0-310-57421-8

Available at your local Christian bookstore.

ZondervanPublishingHouse
Grand Rapids, Michigan

A Division of HarperCollinsPublishers

http://www.zondervan.com